EDWARD ARNOLD

100 Years of Publishing

Edward Arnold 1857–1942 (by Courtesy of Mrs Ireland).

EDWARD ARNOLD

100 Years of Publishing

BRYAN BENNETT
ANTHONY HAMILTON

Edward Arnold

A division of Hodder & Stoughton
LONDON   MELBOURNE   AUCKLAND

© 1990 Bryan Bennett and Anthony Hamilton

First published in Great Britain 1990

British Library Cataloguing in Publication Data

Edward Arnold (Publishers)
  One hundred years of publishing.
  I. Great Britain Publishing Industries. Business Firms hstory
  I. Title   II. Bennett, Bryan   III. Hamilton, Anthony
  338.76107050941

  ISBN 0 340 54109 1

Photoset in Linotron Bembo by Rowland Phototypesetting
Limited, Bury St Edmunds, Suffolk. Printed in Great Britain for
Edward Arnold, a division of Hodder and Stoughton Limited,
Mill Road, Dunton Green, Sevenoaks, Kent TN13 2YA, by
St Edmundsbury Press Limited, Bury St Edmunds, Suffolk.

Contents

Acknowledgments

The authors have received help from many people in writing this book. In particular they would like to thank David Dunhill, Jock Murray, Mervyn Mills, John Morgan and Laurie Vogel; and Richard Stileman for bringing the story up-to-date.

They also wish to thank Philip Attenborough and the Board of Hodder and Stoughton for their invitation to write the book, and for their generosity in giving away a very large proportion of the first printing.

Bryan Bennett
Anthony Hamilton
August 1990

1

The Beginnings

EDWARD AUGUSTUS ARNOLD was born into a family of upper middle-class Victorians who were high-minded and radical, literary and industrious, concerned with education and politics, home-loving yet intrepid travellers, clerical and military, and full of patriotism and Empire. His grandfather was Dr Thomas Arnold, the great public school reformer. Dr Arnold's wife, Mary Penrose, came from a family alive with admirals and vicars.

As well as being "a prophet among schoolmasters", Dr Arnold was also a Victorian paterfamilias and he and Mary had nine children. Five were boys, of whom four were in some way concerned with education.

Matthew Arnold, the eldest, was the poet, Oxford Professor of Poetry and Inspector of Schools. Thomas (Tom) was an Inspector of Schools in Tasmania from 1850 to 1856. He grappled continuously with religious questions; he moved to the Roman Catholic Church in 1856, back to the Anglican Church in 1865 and finally, back again to the Roman faith in 1876. He was Professor of English at Dublin University. His eldest daughter was the novelist, Mrs Humphrey Ward.

The third son was Edward Penrose, described by Mrs H. O. Arnold Forster as "a man highly gifted and remembered with undying love by two generations of friends". He too was an Inspector of Schools, in Devon and Cornwall, and, although somewhat eclipsed by his more dazzling brother Matthew, he performed a great service to education. Much more would have been heard of him had he not died early, aged 51, in 1878. Edward's only son, born on 5 July 1857 at Plymouth, was Edward Augustus

Arnold, who was to found his own publishing company in 1890.

William Delafield, Dr Arnold's fourth son, was an able soldier and administrator, who became Director of Public Instruction in the Punjab at the early age of 28. His interesting novel, *Oakfield* (1853), drew an intense picture of a young radical Arnold's reaction to the British Army in India. He died prematurely aged 31. The fifth son, Walter, served for a few years in the Royal Navy and then became a member of Lloyd's.

The eldest of Dr Arnold's daughters was Jane. She married W. E. Forster, who was responsible for the 1870 Education Act. As A. L. Rowse writes, "The Arnolds (Matthew and his brother Edward) had a decisive influence in forming this great Act – and this was partly exerted very close at hand through their favourite sister, Jane". When William died in 1859, Jane immediately took responsibility for his three children. One of them was Hugh Oakley Arnold, who, with his brothers and sisters, later took the name Arnold-Forster. He became an educational author of note, a director of the publishers Cassell & Company, an MP and eventually Secretary of State for War.

From such a background it is not surprising that Edward Arnold should have chosen to adopt a career in publishing, nor that his own list should have taken the direction it did. Moreover, even in those possibly more gentlemanly days, industry was called for and the Dr Arnold ethic of "'Work' – not work at this or that – but Work!" must have been engraved on the young Edward's mind.

The young Edward Arnold seems to have led a happy boyhood, both at his own home in the West Country and also with his uncles, aunts and cousins at Fox How in the Lake District. The house was originally built by Dr Arnold and, after his death, graciously presided over by Mary Arnold, Edward's grandmother, and then by his great aunt, Fan.

In 1871 Edward went to Eton, possibly because the family felt that the quality of teaching at Rugby had fallen. He enjoyed his years at Eton and reported to his housemaster, J. J. Hornby, that he liked Eton better than Oxford. Mr Hornby was not surprised – "it is easy to construct an argument in favour of the overwhelming superiority of Eton." He matriculated at Corpus Christi in October 1876 and went on to Hertford College, where he graduated with honours in *literae humaniores* in 1880.

Other than his degree, there are no records of Edward's academic or intellectual pursuits at Oxford; but two presentation pewter mugs testify to his sporting interests and successes. The first, dated 1876 from Eton, records that he was the "Winner of The House in the ¼ Mile Handicap, 2nd in putting the weight, 3rd in the House hundred yards". The second, also dated 1876, comes from Corpus Christi College and records that he rowed bow in the winning boat of the Challenge Fours. Throughout his life, Arnold continued to enjoy the outdoor life – especially fishing and sailing in Norway – which no doubt led to his publishing a considerable number of sporting books, mainly concerned with field sports, sailing and climbing.

According to his grandson, the Reverend Robin Dunhill, on leaving Oxford Edward worked for a time as a market gardener – his grandson is not certain where, nor for how long. He does, however, recall that it was during this time that his grandfather decided on publishing as a profession because "it put together his good education and literary background with his attraction towards a business career". This short spell in market gardening, perhaps, caused Edward Arnold to add gardening to the subjects in his early list.

In 1883 or 84 he joined the publishing firm of Richard Bentley, where he learned many aspects of the publishing trade, including up-to-date production techniques. In a letter to John Murray in 1886 he says, "I have never been able to understand the dogma which divorces illustrations from high-class literary matter in a Magazine, except upon the supposition that Editors seldom unite literary attainments with a study of the mechanical processes of Art". Richard Bentley had been one of Dickens's early publishers and had gone on to become one of the leading publishers of the Victorian "three-decker" novels. The business was absorbed by Macmillan's in 1900. At Bentley's, Arnold managed "the country department", which looked after the customers outside London, and later the company's advertising. While there he also edited a volume of Lord Randolph Churchill's speeches – *Plain Politics for the Working Classes*, and took the editorship of the magazine of the Imperial Federation League, whose first Chairman was W. E. Forster and first Secretary H. O. Arnold-Forster. During this period Edward formed the view that there was room for a new national magazine. After much careful research and taking sound-ings from his wide circle of family and friends, he was ready to put a proposal to John Murray. He chose Murray, one of the leading literary publishers of the time, because Murray already published the prestigious *Quarterly Review*, to which Matthew Arnold contributed, and therefore might consider favourably taking on a magazine which would complement the *Quarterly*.

He wrote to Mr Murray on 21 May 1886 asking him to undertake a new Shilling magazine. He argued cogently for the market niche between 2s 6d and 6d, that he had much practical experience, that he would spend freely to obtain the best contributors, that he had a good circle of literary acquaintances and that his "name was known as that of a good literary family". He was able to furnish a list of promised literary support and of course, testimonials. One of these, coming from his cousin the famous novelist and philanthropist Mrs Humphrey Ward, may not have been wholly unprejudiced, but it is nonetheless impressive. She wrote:

> You know the *business* part of the matter thoroughly: which is more than can be said for nine out of ten of the London Editors. You are a man of business yourself, should not shilly shally with your contributors, lose their MSS, and break your promises to them, as too many Editors do.
>
> You have a keen eye for the course of public affairs; and if you are a little more conservative than I am, you are not too conservative for the mass of readers.
>
> You have an inherited interest in literature, and an inherited literary trait.
>
> And lastly, you have activity, and a power of 'pushing' without being a bore.

John Murray hesitated and Edward Arnold continued to " 'push' without being a bore". He presented a market profile of the competitors; his new magazine would make available to a new class of reader, politics, Social subjects and high-class literature. He "would always have at call a few smart writers for a well-presented article, at the shortest possible notice, upon any subject which might suddenly come into prominence". He listed a number of names for the first two issues, including Matthew Arnold, Mrs H. Ward, Randolph Churchill, Robert Browning, the Earl of

Carnarvon, Frank Benson and possibly Henry James. Finally Edward offered to finance the start of the magazine himself, to share the risk with Murray, or to discuss any terms which Murray might propose.

In June 1886 John Murray agreed to what he called "to a certain extent a leap in the dark" and an agreement was made for what was to be *Murray's Magazine* financed by Murray and with Edward Arnold as Editor. The first issue was to appear early in 1887. After one year the Magazine was doing well and in John Murray's view was "of a very high standard". As was to be expected, it made a small financial loss, but this did not prevent John Murray from making a gift of a silver service to Edward Arnold as a token of appreciation for all his hard work. Arnold wrote thanking Murray, expressing his delight upon opening "parcel after parcel of glittering silver!"

In 1888, while continuing energetically to edit *Murray's Magazine*, Arnold also continued as editor of the *Imperial Federation*, edited one or two books for Murray's and began to consider taking on personally the agency in the UK for one of the foremost US educational publishers Ginn & Company of Boston and New York. Nevertheless, he was looking for more work and had discussions with John Murray whereby he might take over management of Murray's advertising department, which was finally offered to him at £200 per year. However there seems to have been some misunderstanding between the Murrays and Arnold over his own arrangements. Arnold was to give up editing the *Imperial Federation* but this Lord Rosebery was reluctant to allow. This fact, and because it was not clear where the Ginn agency was leading to, persuaded Murray to make alternative arrangements for the advertising department. Arnold was disappointed, but amicable relations with Murray's were maintained.

In 1889 as Editor of *Murray's Magazine* Arnold turned down the chance of publishing Thomas Hardy's *Tess of the D'Urbervilles*, which Tillotsons had just withdrawn from as they were "taken aback" by the story. Arnold wrote to Hardy,

> When I had the pleasure of seeing you some time ago, I told you my views about publishing stories where the plot involves frequent and detailed reference to immoral situations: I know well enough

that these tragedies are being played out every day in our midst, but I believe the less publicity they have the better, and it is quite possible and very desirable to grow up and pass through life without knowledge of them. I know your views are different, and I honour your motives.

This was not only the prevailing Victorian view, but one which Arnold continued to hold throughout his publishing life; and he continued to express himself to authors with the same courtesy.

In the same year Murray's reviewed the progress of the *Magazine* and were perfectly happy to write off the accumulated loss of £2700 and to renew Arnold's editorship at 15 guineas per month. In October Arnold again demonstrated his self-confidence by asking John Murray, "quite plainly in a matter of this sort" whether there was any likelihood of his being taken into partnership. If there were not to be any such prospects, then Arnold said that "I should probably try to build up a little business of my own, for beginning which, the present is a good opportunity". John Murray replied the next day: "There is no prospect of a vacancy occurring in the membership of our firm, and I hope it may be long before any vacancy does occur". If matters had been ordered differently, the authors of this history and all their former colleagues would have led very different lives.

Clearly this response did not altogether surprise Arnold, for in the next month he submitted to John Murray the draft of a short circular asking him permission to quote Murray's name "to help in establishing my claim to respectability".

The draft read:

> Mr. Edward A Arnold will remove on January 1st 1890, from 57 & 59 Ludgate Hill, to more convenient and extensive premises at 18 Warwick Square, Paternoster Row EC, where he proposes to carry on the business of a Publisher and Importer of Foreign and American books.
>
> The European business of Messrs Ginn & Company, the well-known Educational publishers of Boston & New York will also be transferred to the above address, and Mr. Arnold will continue to act as their English representative.
>
> Mr. Arnold hopes that his American connections will be of great service to English authors who desire to secure a market for their books in the United States, and also to purchasers of American

books & periodicals who require any information or a means of prompt supply.

Special attention will be given to the Educational Department, with the two-fold object of introducing approved foreign books to English Schools and approved English books to foreign schools.

Reference is permitted to Mr. John Murray; Messrs. R. Bentley & Son; Messrs. Trübner & Co; Messrs. Simpkin Marshall Hamilton Adams Kent & Co; and to Messrs. W. Clowes & Sons.

John Murray agreed and, although it was further agreed that Arnold should continue as Editor of *Murray's Magazine*, his own new business meant that he had to resign after the April number in 1890. So ended the formal link with Murray's, but thereafter, for a hundred years, a special friendship and mutual co-operation existed between the two houses.

Edward Arnold in his twenties.

2

1890–1899

IT was on 1 January 1890 that the English Representative of Ginn & Co., Edward Arnold, moved from a room at Trübners, 57/59 Ludgate Hill, and became Mr Edward Arnold, Publisher at 18 Warwick Square, Paternoster Row, E.C. He retained the Ginn sole agency until 1902, by which time no doubt his own list occupied all of his time.

Arnold showed typical acumen in seeing that "the present is a good opportunity" for starting his own business. In the early 1880s there were about fifty or so publishers, mainly in London. There were the two University presses and a number of companies of many years' standing such as Longman (1724), John Murray (1768), A. & C. Black (1807), Chapman and Hall (1830) and Macmillan (1843). Hodder & Stoughton had come later – in the late 60s. Happily all of these firms are still publishing. The reading public had grown considerably during the previous three decades owing to the dramatic increase of the commercial classes; furthermore the 1870 Elementary Education Act not only provided a larger market for school books but also a new instrument for increasing literacy generally. Some idea of this growth can be seen from one simple statistic: in 1850 about 2600 new books were published, in 1900 there were about 6000.

An opportunity therefore presented itself for some new blood. Between 1885 and 1890 seven new businesses were started: T. Fisher Unwin (1885), George Hutchinson (1887), J. M. Dent (1888), Algernon Methuen (1889) and in 1890 Edward Arnold, Archibald Constable and William Heinemann. The importance of those new companies in the trade at the time can be seen by the fact that they made up seven out of the fifty-eight publishers (12 per cent) who founded the Publishers' Association in 1896. The names of all those seven continue to exist but as lists in, or parts of, larger organizations – Edward Arnold was the last to lose its independence.

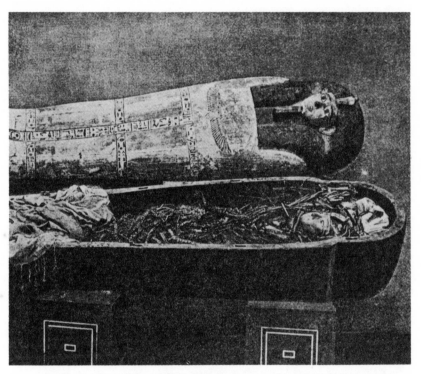

An illustration of the coffin of Amenhotep I from Lynch *Egyptian Sketches*, Edward Arnold's first publication. The book, of 256 pages with 16 plates, was not completed until "the first months of the present year" but was still published on April 24 of the same year, 1890.

For four years Arnold financed and ran the business on his own. At the beginning he took on Mr T. Edward as manager and Mr H. Clifford as traveller, both of whom remained with the company until the 1920s. Presumably there were one or two clerks to deal with orders and to copy the hand-written letters, and also some packers. It is clear, however, that Arnold was responsible for all

9

the publishing, much of the production and he also wrote most of the promotional material.

In May 1890 Arnold was in touch with James Burn, the binders, about one of his early books, mentioned below, *Lamb's Ulysses*. Burns sent a memorandum to Arnold:

> *Lamb's Ulysses*. For 2½d per copy extra we could give you gilt top, title of book, back and side, and picture in gold.
>
> For 3d per copy extra we could give you the same with gilt edges and also the ring round the picture in gold.

Much later, in 1909, we see the hand of Arnold himself at work with the same binding company. The practice of blocking elaborate designs on the book cases, to be covered by "glassine" wrappers or by wrappers on which the binding brasses were printed, was disappearing. Instead, coloured printed wrappers were to be supplied by the publisher. The first such wrapper used by James Burn was for an Arnold book: *The Mystery of the Yellow Room* by Gaston Leroux. Arnold's interest in book production and design is further shown in the promotional piece he wrote giving reasons for his decision to re-issue a library edition of this successful work, not orginally published by him.

> . . . it may be confidently expected to prove the same wonderful success in this edition as in the cheap sixpenny issue which made such an impression upon a section of the public not repelled by small type and paper covers.

Working on his own, now as "Publisher", Mr Edward Arnold needed to produce some books quickly for publication in 1890 and it is unlikely that there would have been any manuscripts sitting in his room at Trübners. Naturally, he would have looked for authors from his own family circle, to magazine contacts and to potential schoolbook writers.

In April 1890 Arnold published his first book, J. Lynch *Egyptian Sketches*, a handsome, well-illustrated demy octavo book of 228 pages at 10s 6d, about which the *Times* said ". . . it is long since we have met with a book on Egypt at once so fresh and so comprehensive". Its first printing was 1500 copies and a reprint of 500 was placed in November of the same year. The author was a member of the Californian State Senate and may have been a *Murray's Magazine* contact.

Arnold's next title, published in May 1890, was provided by his cousin, H. O. Arnold-Forster, but for some reason was published anonymously. Entitled *A Handbook to the Report of the Special Commission*, 5000 copies of this 128 page book were printed and published at 1s. It sold well and was well reviewed. The Attorney-General Sir Richard Webster was quoted: "It seems to me to be very well done. There is nothing of greater importance than the electors of the United Kingdom should understand exactly the effect of the findings of the Judges".

Also in May appeared a medical book for the general reader, *The Modern Malady* by Cyril Bennett, which, for 6s, dealt with "the Nineteenth Century disease commonly known as 'Nerves' ".

During the year, Arnold laid the foundations of his very long line of successful schoolbooks. He published five out of a seven book arithmetic course written by Mr R. Lishman, the Headmaster of the Belle-Vue Higher Board School, Bradford. The five books, ranging from 32 to 40 pages, were each published at 2d. The other two were published in 1891 and the whole series, *The Concrete Arithmetics* Standards I–VII, was welcomed by various HMIs. Naturally they were accompanied by Answer Books – the bane of the educational publisher. Arnold had already learnt that a good schoolbook publisher pays particular attention to Scotland and so, simultaneously, published *The Scottish Concrete Arithmetics*, "the matter being arranged to suit the Standards of the Scotch Code". The books were reprinted yearly, sometimes twice yearly, for many years, were in print until the early 1920s and are remembered today by educational writers such as Leonard Marsh. One obvious way to get a school list established is to publish known classics and so *Lamb's Adventures of Ulysses* with an Introduction by Andrew Lang appeared in May in two editions, ordinary cloth at 1s 6d and "specially bound, with gilt edges, etc." at 2s 6d. Published in May, the book was reprinted in November and remained in print until 1939.

Towards the end of the year the first three titles in the famous *Arnold's English Literature Series* were published by arrangement with Messrs Chapman & Hall. These books were adapted and edited by J. H. Yoxall from Dickens's *David Copperfield, Dombey*

& Son and *The Old Curiosity Shop*. Eventually there were some twenty titles in the *ELS* (fondly remembered by the present authors) most of which remained in print until 1950. One of the two most successful titles in the series was Younghusband's *Epic of Everest*, which only lost its popularity after Everest had finally been climbed, and *The Ascent of Everest* published in 1953. The other was Meade Falkner's *Moonfleet*, of which the *ELS* edition sold many thousands every year throughout the world and which only went out of print in 1974.

Recalling conversations, many years ago, with a few members of the staff who had worked for Arnold, none ever indicated to us that he had a sense of humour – although his correspondence with Professor Sir Walter Raleigh suggests he may have had. In any event, Arnold published in July 1890 Horace Hutchinson's *My Wife's Politics*, which *The Scotsman* described as "a rattle-pated story, full of a delightful, easy-going humour". For many years thereafter Arnold was to have in his list a small but successful section of humorous books, including the classic *Ruthless Rhymes*. The last book published in 1890, of an entirely different nature, was *Animal Life and Intelligence* written by C. Lloyd Morgan, who was Professor at University College, Bristol and an FRS. Arnold was punctilious in clearing this work with John Murray, as the author had written articles for Arnold as editor of *Murray's Magazine* – needless to say, John Murray graciously disclaimed any rights in the work. The book was a success, reprinted in 1891 and later in the same year had a second edition. It was the first scientific work in a long list of important and substantial textbooks and monographs published by the company over the following hundred years. Morgan himself wrote another four books on biological and psychological topics over the next six years, all of which had many reprints and new editions and remained in print for periods from twenty-five to thirty years.

In his first year Mr Edward Arnold, Publisher, not only continued to represent throughout the UK the very large Ginn school and university list, ranging from simple readers to works on Anglo-Saxon and Sanskrit, but managed himself to bring out eleven school books and five general books.

In his 1890 catalogue he listed his own and Ginn's books and further announced that he had arrangements with the leading

A CATALOGUE

OF

EDUCATIONAL WORKS

PUBLISHED AND SOLD BY

MR. EDWARD ARNOLD,

INCLUDING THOSE OF

MESSRS. GINN & COMPANY,

BOSTON AND NEW YORK.

LONDON:

EDWARD ARNOLD,

18, WARWICK SQUARE, PATERNOSTER ROW, E.O.

July, 1890.

The first known catalogue from Mr Edward Arnold

American and Continental publishers for the supply of books and periodicals "FORWARDED BY THE FIRST MAIL STEAMER leaving New York or Boston, no matter how small the parcel". Who would say that in 1990?

In 1891 Arnold maintained his impetus and published ten general books and seven school books. In the middle of the year he moved his office and took more commodious premises at 37, Bedford Street – the move did not seem to interfere seriously with his publishing programme. He published another book by Horace Hutchinson – *That Fiddler Fellow* – which was a humorous golfing story set in St Andrews and which stayed popular for some fifteen years. He also began his gardening list by bringing back into print Dean S. R. Hole's *A Book About Roses*. Arnold issued the eleventh edition and the book, whose fifteenth edition was published in 1896, continued to charm gardeners until the 1920s. Hole wrote another book for Arnold in 1892 – *About the Garden and the Gardeners* – which was in demand until the Great War. Dean Hole also wrote several books of memoirs and travel during the next few years. Despite Arnold's interest in gardens, Joe Greener, of whom more later, remembered that in about 1912, when he had just started as an office boy, he was asked by his formidable employer "Are you interested in gardening?" Joe replied brightly that he was. "Good" replied Arnold, "but don't bring it into the office with you!" Joe was wearing a rose in his buttonhole.

Two other significant books were published in 1891. *My Mission to Abyssinia*, by Sir Gerald Porter, was the first of a long line of books, many very important, dealing with political and gubernatorial matters and reminiscences; this was followed in 1894 by his second book, *The British Mission to Uganda*. The other work was Arnold's first novel. Mrs W. R. Clifford, already a successful author, was persuaded to place her new epistolary novel, *Love Letters of a Worldly Woman* with Edward Arnold. It ran through ten impressions and a cheap edition was published in 1908.

Also in 1891 Arnold extended his activities by becoming Publisher to the India Office, an appointment which lasted until 1911. Books and maps published by the Government of India were not listed separately but were available either from 37 Bedford Street or "at the shortest possible notice".

During 1892 Arnold, while continuing his general list, increased his educational output to twenty-four books in the year. He did this by adapting certain Ginn titles, by taking over books already issued by schoolmasters and adding new ones, for example those written by R. Wormell, Headmaster of the Central Foundation School in London, and by starting a number of series of Arnold readers. The Arnold series were to cover English Language and Literature, Geography, History, the Bible, Domestic Science and Drawing. They covered all levels and were priced from twopence to one shilling and sixpence. By 1900 there were over 200 titles available, and many of them in paper and cloth versions. History does not tell us who the authors or editors were; some of the books were no doubt created in-house and others written by teachers on a fee basis. All of these series lasted for many years. Over the years they were joined by further series covering Latin, French and German. In 1939 there were still about 370 titles in print from the various series, although by then the prices ranged from twopence (still!) to two shillings and ninepence. Most of the later books had named authors and editors.

1892 saw the publication of Arnold's first religious book, written by Bell, and entitled, *The Name Above Every Name*, a collection of sermons, and his first history book *The Battles of Frederick the Great*, edited by Professor C. Ransome from Carlyle's work.

An extraordinarily popular book was Charles Santley's *Student and Singer, Reminiscences*. Santley, an opera singer of international repute, was later knighted for his services to opera. Published in October, second and third editions were published in November and a fourth edition in December. It is a surprise, therefore, to see that his two later books of 1908 and 1909 were not published by Arnold.

One of Arnold's most seminal books was also published in 1892; written by Alfred, later Viscount, Milner, *England in Egypt* became an instant success. Published in December, it was reprinted in January, February and April the following year. A new edition was published in May 1894; various editions followed over the years and the last edition in the UK, the thirteenth, appeared in 1920. In 1970 the work was still considered important enough to be re-published by Howard Fertig Inc. in New York. The *Dictionary of National Biography* says "But probably the greatest service that Milner rendered to his country's task in Egypt was by his book

England in Egypt, written in six months" in which he makes the case that England can best help Egypt by "helping the Egyptians to do for themselves". Milner was greatly influenced by Arnold Toynbee and wrote a book on him, published by Arnold in 1895, a second edition of which appeared in 1901 and was to continue in print until the 1920s. *The Times* described it as "A masterly analysis of a commanding personal influence".

The warm relationship which Arnold maintained with Milner over many years was typical of that which he enjoyed with many of his authors. On 29 March 1925, Milner wrote in answer to Arnold's birthday letter. He refers to his reminiscences, which he looked forward to doing if he had "a further span of years left" and would not be attracted by "a very big offer made by one of your chief competitors". He was delighted that *England in Egypt* was still alive and added "I think you managed it very well, for which I am grateful". Sadly, he died six weeks later, just after being named as Chancellor-elect of Oxford University.

During 1892 Arnold began another important series. Starting by taking quires from Appleton, New York, he issued the first two volumes of *The International Education Series*, which by 1900 numbered fifty titles including edited works by Rousseau, Froebel, Dickens and Adler. The arrangement with Appleton came to an end in 1904 (perhaps on Arnold's removal to Maddox Street) but Arnold went on to create two series of his own – *Arnold's Educational Classics* and *The Modern Educator's Library*, both of which lasted for many years. The most famous book in the latter series, *Education: Its Data and First Principles* by Professor T. Percy Nunn, published in 1920, remained in print until the 1970s.

An accident had occurred in the winter of 1892, whose outcome was to determine the future of this history. Edward Arnold and his wife had gone skating on Virginia Water with his cousin Arnold-Forster and his wife. Edward fell through the ice in the middle of the lake and Arnold-Forster could not reach him, even with a ladder he had procured, as the ice kept giving way and Arnold-Forster himself went under the water. He managed to get out but even with ropes could not reach Edward, who had now been in the freezing water for some time. Arnold-Forster offered a reward of £10 to any young lad of very light weight who would volunteer, properly roped to the bystanders, to get a rope to

Edward. A volunteer was found and eventually a frozen and exhausted Edward was got out just in time. Arnold-Forster and the boy were awarded Royal Humane Society medals for their bravery, and Edward Arnold recovered to resume his publishing career.

Significant publications in 1893 were *The Cultivation and Use of Imagination* by J. G., later Viscount, Goschen, a former Chancellor of the Exchequer, who also later wrote *Essays and Addresses on Economic Questions 1865–95*, published in 1905; W. E. H. Lecky *The Political Value of History*; and an extremely popular book of reminiscences by W. R. Le Fanu *Seventy Years of Irish Life*. This title reprinted twice in the year, followed by other reprints and a new edition in 1896. The later Popular Edition remained in print until the late 1940s.

In 1893 Arnold published seventeen general titles and forty school and teachers' books.

At some time in 1894 Arnold took into partnership Mr A. L. Mumm – a member of the champagne family – who had been a friend of Arnold's at Eton and who had been called to the bar. *T. P.'s Weekly* described him to be, like Arnold, "an open-air man". Mumm was certainly a great climbing man; he was Honorary Secretary of the Alpine Club and was later its Vice-President. He was to write in 1909 *Five Months in the Himalaya* describing the expedition he undertook together with Major Bruce and Dr Longshaft. The latter reached the summit of Trisul 23415 feet above sea level, then the highest point on earth "that had been trodden by man".

It is not clear just how much Mumm was involved in day-to-day publishing. Those who worked for the company in the 1900s always referred to him as a sleeping partner, but there is evidence that he undertook some editorial functions and also sought authors. It is fairly certain that Mumm, through his connections, started the mountaineering list which flourished until the 1930s and which included many classics. The first title to appear was the extremely successful *Exploration of the Caucasus* by D. W. Freshfield, published in July 1896. It was a splendid production in two volumes with many fine photographs. The limited edition was five guineas and the standard edition three guineas – Arnold's most expensive books for about twenty years. A cheap edition was published in 1902, with no plates, for only one guinea; it remained in print until the 1920s.

In 1894 Arnold moved into cookery books, issuing two titles: A. Kenny Herbert *Fifty Breakfasts* followed by *Commonsense Cookery*. A curiously modern note is struck in the author's preface to the second book, where he writes "Another cookery book! Yes – another! Surely there can be none too many if each contribute but a little in aid of the movement now fairly on foot for the betterment of English cookery". In those far off days, the level of writing was often higher than now. It was a list which, in various forms, continues successfully to the present. He also published his second poetry book by the Reverend Canon A. Bell, entitled *Diana's Looking Glass and Other Poems*. The original poetry list went on for some years in a genteel sort of way – mainly polite, religious or imperial verse – but it would be fair to say that Edward had not inherited his Uncle Matthew's poetical or critical gifts. More to Edward's liking was the first of a long line of sporting books, H. Custance: *Riding Recollections and Turf Stories*. Published in January, it was reprinted in the same month, followed by a new edition in May, which also reprinted in the same month. In total there were nineteen general books and twenty-one schoolbooks, including the first of *Arnold's School Shakespeare* – *A Midsummer Night's Dream*, edited by J. Churton Collins, published in 1894. The series remained in print until the late 1940s.

At this time Arnold, in common with other UK publishers, was suffering from the US copyright laws. In order to qualify for protection of copyright in the USA, it was necessary that the books themselves should be "manufactured" in the USA, a situation which lasted until 1907. Arnold set up a New York office in 1895, at 70, Fifth Avenue. There are no records to show what its organization was or who ran it. Like most other things at this time, it appears that Arnold himself was responsible for it while it existed from 1895 to early 1898.

In some cases Arnold published books in New York which were not also published by him in London. Such books were Charles Allen, *Papier Mâché* (1896), Grant Allen: *An African Millionaire* (1897) and H. G. Wells: *The Invisible Man* and *Thirty Strange Stories* (also 1897). In the same year he also published in New York Hilaire Belloc's *Bad Child's Book of Beasts*, which had been originally published in England by Alden & Co., Oxford, and in London another book by Belloc: *More Verse for Worse Children*. This title, however, did not bear the joint imprint of London and New York, and it is not clear what happened to it in the USA.

THIRTY
STRANGE STORIES

BY

H. G. WELLS

Author of "The Time Machine," "The Wheels of Chance,"
"The Wonderful Visit," Etc.

Cloth, 12mo, 500 pp.   -   - $1.50.

"Creepy, ingenius, original and more than clever they all are. They fascinate you like the eye of a snake....... It would be impossible to find a group of stories that will give the reader more sensations, or hold his attention more firmly."—*Boston Herald*.

"They are strange stories, fully out of the ruts, wierd, realistic and fascinating, and often with a rich, quiet humor."—*Chicago Inter-Ocean*.

"All the stories are strange, some of them instinct with humor and others have a tragic note. The collection is a remarkable one." —*Chicago Journal*.

"Stands out by reason of its humor, freshness and originality as a thing to be grateful for........ Mr. Wells has humor keen and unforced, great imaginative power, and a substantial basis of thorough scientific knowledge, and his style is in general natural and polished, while his versatility is shown in the wide range of these stories."—*N. Y. Sun*.

"Few living writers have carried the art of telling short stories to such a high degree of perfection as Mr. Wells, and this collection shows him at his best."—*San Francisco Argonaut*.

"The application of the fascinatingly curious things in science to the uses of fiction has never before been so successfully made as by Mr. Wells. To effect the uncanny, the grotesque and the humorous he brings to his aid the oddities of the air, the sea, the world of animals and the fourth dimension. Mr. Wells is at all times essentially readable, and this collection of tales shows a far better average of entertainment than any volume an American magazine could produce. Reading them, I wonder why the people who are perpetually complaining that all the stories worth telling were told long years ago do not, as does Mr. Wells, take advantage of the constant discoveries in modern science and industry and use them for fiction."—*Town Topics*.

One of Arnold's leaflets produced by or for the New York office in 1897.

In other cases Arnold did publish simultaneous editions such as *George's Mother* by Stephen Crane, author of *The Red Badge of Courage*, and this book was printed in the USA. It is also likely that Arnold tried the stratagem of binding UK sheets in New

York to qualify for "manufacture" in the USA. An entry in the publication ledger shows that half the sheets of *Fire and Sword in the Sudan* were lost on *SS Cephalonia* and had to be reprinted in 1896; the book had a joint imprint of London and New York.

Presumably Arnold's efforts in the USA were not eventually felt by him to be worth persevering with, because the New York office and the joint imprint were dispensed with in 1898. The problem of US copyright remained and Professor, later Sir Walter, Raleigh, who maintained a most amusing correspondence with Arnold throughout their long association, wrote about his book *Milton* in 1900:

> What I should like you to do is this. Print twenty copies and publish them in America at $15 a copy. Perhaps these would sell, perhaps more, for there are many rich and eccentric collectors. I would of course pay for this edition. Further, I would prefix to it a copy of verses entitled "To the People of America". This proposal is serious.

Whether it was or not, the proposal was not pursued, but later in the year an edition was licensed to Putnam. It was to be eighty-four years before Edward Arnold was to have another branch in the USA.

Meanwhile in London in 1895 Arnold continued building his list with thirty-two general and eighteen schoolbooks. The general list was expanded by adding eleven works of fiction. It also included the first of Walter Raleigh's critical works: *Robert Louis Stevenson*; published in October, it reprinted the following January. At the time Raleigh was Professor of English Literature at University College, Liverpool. He then held the chair at Glasgow University and in 1904 was appointed to the new chair of English Literature at Oxford; he was knighted in 1911. He was a lucid, lively writer who had the gift of transferring his enthusiasms to the reader. He was also an extremely amusing man in conversation and in his letters, but could be self-deprecating. He wrote three other books for Arnold, *Style* (1897), *Milton* (1900) and *Wordsworth* (1903). He died in 1922 and in 1926 Arnold published *On Writing and Writers*, Raleigh's longer lecture notes edited by George Gordon. All Raleigh's five titles became quickly established and remained in print until the early 1950s. In all of Raleigh's letters cheerfulness keeps breaking out: "my cherished ambition to be a twopenny in the shilling author"; about *Milton* "Much of it, whether true or not, is new" and "I do not try to annoy; but if it is my fate, this is a compensation"; about his own book *Style*, "It was a conceited and stuck-up book", "I believe that the only man who ever attempted to use *Style* as a handbook of literary composition for a College class went mad, and was clapped up in an asylum. Not a word of this to Putnam" (the New York publisher); about an Agreement "I wish it were simpler and modern; in a complicated net there are many bonds but also many loopholes"; about his own book *Wordsworth* "But a criticism (the least popular form of writing) on Bill (the least popular of poets) – where would that lead me?"; about collections "A published lecture is a dead lecture, and I live by lecturing". To publish an outstanding, successful author over a long period, who writes to you in this way, is some reward for the academic publisher.

Of the schoolbooks published in 1895, two stand out. Charles, later Sir Charles, Oman's *A History of England* was published in April and reprinted twice in the following year and at the same time reprinted as two volumes. The *Guardian* described it as "the nearest approach to the ideal School History of England which has yet been written". The *Saturday Review* believed "It will be the standard school book for many years to come" – a sound prophecy for the book lasted for over fifty years. The other book was *French Without Tears* by Mrs Hugh (later Lady) Bell, who had already written some humorous books for Arnold. This charming little book, with its amusing illustrations, followed the "direct method" (to come back in vogue in the 1950s). It was an immediate success, reprinting twice in 1896 and four times in 1897. Two other books followed in 1896 and the three-book course continued to sell well until the 1960s and gave a phrase to the English language. An adaptation was published as *German Without Tears* and this too had a long life, lasting until the 1950s.

In 1896 the rate of publication increased to sixty one books – the highest yearly figure so far. Apart from Mumm, who were the other shadowy figures at work getting these books through? We do not know. However, there were a further eleven novels (including Stephen Crane's already mentioned). The first nursing book was published, an adaptation for the UK of an American book by C. S. Weeks-Shaw, *A Textbook of Nursing*.

The most remarkable publication in 1896 was R. C. Slatin Pasha: *Fire and Sword in the Sudan*, in which the Austrian author tells of his being held captive for twelve years by the Mahdi. About the book the *Spectator* said "Absolutely unique. Were we to try to extract, or even notice, all the striking things in this book we should fill our paper". The story goes that when Arnold was talking to Slatin Pasha, Slatin mentioned that he was forty. Arnold suggested that he should have guessed rather more. "I don't count the twelve years that I was in the Mahdi's camp", was the grim rejoinder. The book was a success: published in January, it reprinted in February and twice in March. It reprinted again in January 1897; a popular edition was published in September 1897 and this reprinted twice in the year. Other reprints followed until 1907 when a revised edition, with no maps, was issued. This edition remained in the list for a further forty years. At the end of the year another climbing book appeared, *In and Beyond the Himalayas* by S. J. Stone, illustrated by the legendary Charles Whymper.

Publication eased a little in 1897 when the output dropped to forty-six books, of which twelve were for schools. A notable addition to the other novelists was Mary Cholmondeley, who had several novels already published elsewhere. Her new book, *A Devotee*, came out in March, at the going price for novels of six shillings, and was reprinted in May. It was, however, only a modest success when compared with her second book for Arnold, *Red Pottage*, which was published two years later and which must have been one of Arnold's biggest-selling novels. Between 1899 and 1901 the book went through thirteen impressions and in 1905 a cheap edition was published at 2s 6d, which remained in print until the 1920s. A licensed edition was also published in 1901 in *Newnes Sixpenny Novels* series – illustrated by the up-and-coming Arthur Rackham. The book was a dramatic and well-told story of love and honour, in which the heroine's unconventional manuscript is thrown on the fire by her outraged clergyman brother. It so happened that the first printing of the book itself sold out immediately. Arnold quickly ordered a reprint, only to learn that the plates had been consumed by a fire at the printers, Ballantyne and Hanson. Arnold and the printer moved swiftly; the fire took place on Saturday night but by Thursday morning the reprint was ready for the impatient public.

Apart from Raleigh's *Style* and Belloc's *More Beasts*, mentioned above, two other books were published in 1897 which reflect the growing diversity of Arnold's list. A new series entitled *Arnold's Practical Science Manuals*, under the general editorship of Professor R. Meldola FRS, was started; its first book, by George Halliday of the Finsbury Technical College, was *Steam Boilers*. The series marked Arnold's entry into engineering texts and monographs, a list which goes on to the present. At the other end of the spectrum was the sumptuous and scholarly work by A. Hartshorne, Fellow of the Society of Antiquaries, *Old English Glasses*. This was a superb royal quarto book, beautifully illustrated, printed and bound, and dedicated by special permission to Her Majesty the Queen. Priced at three guineas, this account of English glass drinking-vessels remained in print until the depression of the 1930s when, priced at five pounds ten shillings, it went out of print. Today it is a collector's item.

1898 saw another forty four books published, of which thirteen were for schools. Of the latter the most interesting was A. J. Herbertson's *An Illustrated School Geography*. This was probably the first attempt to make the illustrations as systematic and import-ant as the text and to integrate the whole. When, in the 1960s, we were justifiably proud of Young and Lowry's revolutionary *Course in World Geography*, we were somewhat chastened when we dis-covered that Herbertson had thought of this approach sixty years before. The book attracted golden opinions, of which the *School Board Chronicle*'s was typical: "Nothing finer in the shape of a modern school-book of geography has ever been published". Curiously, this fine book went out of print in 1903. Priced in two versions, at 5s and 7s 6d, it may be an early proof of the educational publisher's theorem that schools will pay more for something special – but not that much more!

In May, Arnold published his cousin H. O. Arnold-Forster's *Army Letters 1897–98*, being a series of letters reprinted from *The Times*, urging reform of the army. This was greatly welcomed by the army and led Arnold into publishing a number of significant books on the subject of defence up to the 1914 war. Another Belloc book of humorous, illustrated verse was published, *The Modern*

Traveller. All of Belloc's similar books went on until the 1930s, when perhaps the mood of the times or the publisher changed, and they went out of print. They were revived by Duckworth and continue in print today. In the same year another humorous book appeared, *Tails With a Twist* by "A Belgian Hare" and illustrated by E. T. Reid. The "Hare" was the notorious Lord Alfred Douglas, who had just returned from voluntary exile following his association with Oscar Wilde. Douglas sold the copyright to Arnold for £50 and was later reprimanded by Bernard Shaw for so doing. Douglas was often accused of having plagiarised Belloc's *Book of Beasts* (1896) but, as he recorded in later editions of his own work, most of the rhymes had been written two years before Belloc's and were widely known at Oxford, where Belloc was Douglas' contemporary. Does this explain the curious pseudonym, making a play on Belloc's initials and his French name? *Tails With a Twist* had a considerable success on publication and remained in print until 1916, when printing facilities and paper were in short supply.

In November of 1898 Arnold published one of his most successful books, *Moonfleet* by J. Meade Falkner. Falkner was an academic who, almost by accident, went into business and ended up as Chairman of Armstrong, Whitworth the giant armaments company. He then became honorary librarian to the Dean and Chapter of Durham Cathedral and honorary reader in palaeography at Durham University – a unique career. His first book, *The Lost Stradivarius*, had been published in 1895 and it is not clear how Arnold obtained his second book, though probably he would have known Falkner as they were near contemporaries at Hertford College. *Moonfleet* is a classic smuggling romance considered by many to be as good as *Treasure Island*. The book went through many impressions and a cheap edition was published in 1917, remaining in print until 1939. The title was put into the *Arnold's English Literature Series* in 1924 and, as already noted, went on selling many thousands of copies each year until the late 1970s. In 1955 an elegant illustrated library edition was published which itself had several reprints. The book has also been available in Penguin for many years. In 1953 Brian Fagan, the then Chairman, conducted lengthy and complicated negotiations with MGM for a film version. He was invited to the glittering première, only to return as cross as we had ever seen him. "I don't know why they bothered with a contract" he muttered, "this dreadful film has nothing at all to do with the book".

Later, in 1903, Arnold published Falkner's acknowledged masterpiece, *The Nebuly Coat*. Here all his interests: history, architecture, music, heraldry and genealogy all come together in a skilful plot convincingly told. For some reason the book was allowed to go out of print in 1919. However, in 1954 the two titles, *The Lost Stradivarius* and *The Nebuly Coat* appeared together as one volume in *The World's Classics* published by OUP. Falkner also wrote many poems for periodicals; three of them are included in Philip Larkin's *Oxford Book of Twentieth Century Verse*, 1973.

A record was set in 1899 with the publication of seventy four books, but of these many were small Arnold school series books. *Red Pottage* was published in this year and also one of Arnold's remarkably long-lived medical books, *A Manual of Human Physiology* by Leonard, later Sir Leonard, Hill, Hunterian Professor, the Royal College of Surgeons. This text had several editions, the fourth (and last) was published in 1934 and remained in print until the 1950s. Hill was to write a further five medical books for Arnold; one published in 1924 was very much of its time, *Sunshine and Open Air, Their Influence on Health, with Special Reference to the Alpine Climate*. A new edition of this lengthy title went on until the late 1940s.

Another remarkable school book was published this year, Charles Oman's second, *England in the Nineteenth Century*. It was as well received as his first book, the reviewers praising his scholarship, impartiality, patriotism and love of Empire. The book lived until the Empire itself died after 1945. Belloc's *A Moral Alphabet* was published and in the same month appeared *Ruthless Rhymes for Heartless Homes* by "Col D. Streamer". It is unlikely that any reader of this history has not also read or heard some, at least of these rhymes. Not only are they still in print, but no anthology of comic verse can appear without one or two of the rhymes being present (not always acknowledged!).

Here are two of these timeless rhymes which are most often anthologized.

Mr Jones

"There's been an accident!" they said,
"Your servant's cut in half; he's dead!"
"Indeed!" said Mr Jones, "and please
Send me the half that's got my keys."

Tender-Heartedness

Billy, in one of his nice new sashes,
Fell in the fire and was burnt to ashes:
Now, although the room grows chilly,
I haven't the heart to poke poor Billy.

The author was Harry Graham, a well-connected young Captain in the Coldstream Guards – hence his pseudonym, which was soon dropped. He was ADC to the Governor General of Canada, the Earl of Minto, in 1898 and later private secretary to the Earl of Rosebery. He served in the South African War from 1901 to 1902 and again in the 1914–18 war. He wrote several books of comic verse and five other humorous works during the next twenty years and, in 1930, his other masterpiece *More Ruthless Rhymes for Heartless Homes*, the necessary stimulus for which, Graham admitted, was provided by the commissioners of the Inland Revenue. The two books of *Rhymes* have remained in print until today – an edition combining both books was first published in 1984. He also wrote sixteen plays and musicals, the most famous being *White Horse Inn* and *Maid of the Mountains*. Harry Graham acted as a part-time scout for Edward Arnold and then in 1910 was appointed as literary editor, a post which he held until 1914. He was described by Joe Greener as "a very tall Guards officer about 6 foot 8 inches and he was always thought of by the staff as the Perfect Gentleman". He was very well placed to find authors and readers for the growing list of fiction, reminiscences and travel, sport and military books. We can catch glimpses of the man from his correspondence with potential authors. To a Mr Munro, whose book was not published, Graham wrote in 1911 to point out that a suggestion of padding out the proposed book to the required length was not a very useful one: unable to comprehend the morality of the plot, he ended his letter by asking the author "Is it conceivable that any young man would borrow money from the girl he is in love with?" Writing to Sir Sydney Colvin, whose memoirs were published, Graham wrote "No, I do not belong to the Athenaeum, but only to the Garrick, which is rather dingy for strangers!" On his death in 1936 *The Times* said that Graham had "pushed through satire and come out on the other side into a kingdom of nonsense all his own."

By the end of 1899 Arnold had completed his first ten years as publisher. Working very largely on his own, he had published nearly five hundred titles of which 220 were general books and 250 educational. The pattern of his publishing fixed in these ten years was to remain much the same over the next thirty years, even though various other editors and partners were to join him.

The largest section of his list was travel, which numbered some forty titles, followed by biography and reminiscences, numbering thirty-two. Sport and science came next with fourteen titles each, followed by philosophy/religion, humour, politics and literature, all of which were around the dozen. Smaller sections covered history, gardening, cookery and small-holding. In the school list most of the books were on the arts side, with only thirty science and maths titles. The proportion probably reflected the school syllabuses as much as Arnold's own inclinations. His grandson, Robin Dunhill, remembers being told by Arnold that in the early days of the firm he personally visited every likely school in the country to seek out authors. During this period he also continued for some time as the Ginn agent in the UK; he became Publisher to the India Office; he published or acted as agent for, at various times, *The National Review*, *The Westminster Review* and *The Forum*; he had also taken on the publication of the Essex House Press list, limited edition books of high scholarship printed on the late Mr William Morris's Kelmscott presses and designed by C. R. Ashbee. It would appear then that, apart from other Arnold family inheritances, the Dr Arnold belief in the work ethic was genetically transmitted to the grandson.

3

1900–1918

IN the first year of the twentieth century Arnold's output dropped to forty one titles, made up of fifteen general books, seven fiction and nineteen school books. One of the general books, commissioned by Arnold, was Belloc's *Paris*, which A. N. Wilson described as having a strong appeal to the faculty of the historical imagination written in the most elegant prose, but nevertheless a book which did not bring the author much money. Raleigh's *Milton* was published in 1900, as was Arnold's uncle Thomas Arnold's autobiography, *Passages in a Wandering Life*.

An important addition to the medical list was Robert, later Sir Robert, Hutchinson's pioneering work *Food and the Principles of Dietetics*. The book was written to remedy, "the almost total neglect of the subject of dietetics in ordinary education" and it succeeded in doing so. Five reprints appeared before the book went into its second edition in 1905. Thereafter it reprinted yearly and its last edition – the twelfth – was published in 1969, only going out of print in 1980.

Arnold's mathematics list was strengthened in 1901 by the publication of Louis and Caunt's *Traverse Tables*, followed in 1903 by Dale's *Five Figure Tables of Functions* and in 1904 by the same author's *Logarithmic and Trigonometric Tables*. Dale's two books remained in print until the 1970s. *The London School Atlas* appeared in 1901. This was edited by cousin Arnold-Forster, then a director of Cassell's, another educational publisher. Arnold-Forster had already created the *Universal Atlas* for Cassell. This was later to become *The Times Atlas*, the publication of which was taken over by Arnold in 1902 until 1910. Of the *London School Atlas*, published in five versions ranging from 1s 6d to 3s 6d, *Nature* wrote "As a specimen of colour printing, this atlas is the finest thing ever produced or published in this country". It went on, with various revisions, until 1920. (In the 1960s we tried with John Morgan to adapt a new German atlas for the British market – unfortunately it proved too complicated in presentation and too expensive in production for the taste and the pocket of UK schools and was not pursued.)

Another long-lived book first appeared in 1901, written by Florence George of King Edward's School, Birmingham, entitled *King Edward's Cookery Book*. A good, simple and practical book, it was followed in 1908 by a similarly practical book called *Vegetarian Cookery*. Both books proved their practicality by being in demand for over fifty years.

The quality and the rate of publication – about 50 titles per year – were maintained during 1901 and 1902. In the latter year two already successful authors had other books published – Charles Oman: *Seven Roman Statesmen* and Walter Raleigh: *Wordsworth*, both of which remained in print for over fifty years.

Towards the end of 1902, Arnold's growing list led him seriously to think of moving again – this time into a new purpose-built office and warehouse, perhaps the first English publishing house to be so designed. He must have consulted his surveyor and architect in the last few months of 1902 and, early in 1903, plans and negotiations began in earnest. Throughout the year there was copious correspondence leading to many meetings, cancelled meetings and re-appointed meetings.

When the site had been selected, under the London Building Act of 1894 various notices were to be served to sundry owners and occupiers of adjoining premises in Maddox Street, George Street and Bond Street. Ancient Lights were inevitably invoked; party-walls, chimney stacks and telephone standards were the subject of many discussions; a number of architect tracings were examined and the laying of pipes negotiated; legal proceedings were threatened by a neighbour, Sir John Ramsden, whose long absences in Scotland made personal interviews impossible; offers and counter-offers were made for the freehold of the existing buildings (agreed finally at £13000); an advance from Coutts & Co. for £10000 was negotiated; alternative construction costs had to be

The first purpose-built publishing house in London? ". . . the basement is going to be a very fine one".

pored over; objections by the District Surveyors needed to be overruled by the County Council. Completion of the purchase of the premises, to be demolished, at 41/43 Maddox Street took place on 25 March 1903. All the correspondence and meetings with solicitors, surveyors, architects and anyone else were dealt with by Arnold himself. In December the surveyor wrote to Arnold to arrange an inspection, saying "The work is progressing well and the basement is going to be a very fine one". In fact the whole building turned out to be a very fine one and it stands today, although the interior has been much changed and "modernized". There is no record of the cost of the new building, but it was insured through the County Fire Office for £9800.

The move into the new premises took place in May 1904 and Mr Edward Arnold announced his 'Special Removal Sale' to the trade from 14 April to 1 May. The list included only the slower-moving titles and the discounts offered ranged from 50 per cent to 75 per cent.

Despite all this activity, the publishing did not suffer – on the contrary, during 1903/4 output reached new levels with seventy-eight and seventy-five books respectively and by 1905 had reached 101 titles. In 1903 there was Meade Falkner's *The Nebuly Coat* and a book which made quite a splash, *My Memoirs* by H. S. de Blowitz, who was the larger-than-life Paris correspondent of *The Times* for nearly thirty years. It did well and a popular edition was issued in 1906. A more serious and controversial work was L. S. Amery's *The Problem of the Army*. Based on a series of articles in *The Times*, this was another of Arnold's books published before the 1914 war which addressed the need to reform the army in the light of current circumstances.

1904 was marked not only by the move, but by the publication of another distinguished medical book by Robert Hutchison, *Lectures on Diseases of Children*, of which there were nine editions and which lasted for some sixty years. It was also the year in which the first of M. R. James's collections of ghost stories was published. James was then Provost of King's College, Cambridge and a distinguished scholar in medieval studies, palaeography and bibliography. It is thought that the first of his stories were written for the King's choristers. The very first, *The Scrapbook of Canon Alberic* was published in the *National Review* in 1895 (at ten shillings per page!). As publisher of the journal, Arnold wrote to James in 1902, inviting him to write or contribute to a proposed work, *Chapters on the History of Learning in England*. James was keen to be involved but, for various reasons, this work did not materialize. However, James did send about six ghost stories, together with some illustrations by James McBryde, to Arnold in May. Arnold replied enthusiastically but asked James "to extract some more horrors so as to make up the volume to 6/- length". James provided a further two stories by the end of July; the proofs arrived in October and the book was published at the end of November in time for the Christmas trade. Its title was *Ghost Stories of an Antiquary* and it included the most famous of all the stories, "Oh, Whistle, And I'll Come To You My Lad". The book was well designed and bound in hessian-covered yapp boards. It was reprinted in the following year and, together with all James's other stories, remains in print today. In 1911 *More Ghost Stories of an Antiquary* was published and, in 1919, a third volume of only five stories, *A Thin Ghost*. Finally came *A Warning to the Curious*, published in October 1925, and reprinted in November and December. In 1931 all these volumes were published together as the *Collected Ghost Stories* and it is this edition that is still in print. There have been many editions in many parts of the world, including translations. Many of the stories have been adapted for films and television. Most critics, including Michael Cox, believe that M. R. James produced "arguably the finest ghost stories in the English language". In 1922 Arnold published another book by M. R. James. *The Five Jars* was a fantasy for children and, although "a charming curiosity", it did not achieve the success of the ghost stories, but remained in print until the late 1940s. In 1956 James's *Letters to a Friend* was published. These were letters written to Gwendolen McBryde, the widow of the artist.

To return to 1904. Immediately after the move, Arnold achieved a minor coup in persuading T. Cowen, who was the special correspondent of the *News Chronicle* to write *The Russo-Japanese War*, an account of the first campaigns. It was advertised as being "in rapid preparation". Within twenty-three days of receipt of the manuscript the book, which had 344 pages of text and 34 pages of maps and illustrations, was in the bookshops at fifteen shillings.

As *TP's Weekly* put it "it depended enormously on being prompt – on hitting the public when it is interested in a subject". The interest was further indulged in 1905 with the publication of Sir Ian Hamilton's *A Staff Officer's Scrap-book During the Russo-Japanese War*.

A new dimension was added to the travel list in 1905 by the publication of two particularly interesting books. The first was Edmund Candler's *The Unveiling of Lhasa*. The author was the Special Correspondent of the *Daily Mail* with the famous Tibet Mission. Edward Arnold had some difficulty in corresponding with Candler in 1904 as the address was simply "Tibet Mission". However letters did get through both ways, although the "Press Censorship was unnecessarily strict". Some idea of the discomfort undergone by the author is revealed in his apology to Arnold: "Please excuse pencil, ink freezes". The book was reprinted three times in 1905 and continued in print until the 1914 War. The second title was *Two Years in the Antarctic*, written by A. B. Armitage, who had been Second-in-Command of the *Discovery* from 1901 to 1904. The book was in print until the second expedition in 1911. Armitage did not go on that expedition and Arnold wrote to Scott in 1910 seeking a book. Scott explained that he had already made arrangements for the publication of his next book and ended his letter by saying "I remember meeting you very well and regret there will not be more than one book". Tragically, although Scott's diaries were published, there was not even one book.

The level of publication remained high in 1906 with a total of ninety-two books, of which fifty were for schools, but it dropped to only fifty-five titles in the following year, of which twenty-eight were school books. The mix of titles followed the pattern now set for the last few years and included another of the medical titles which was to last for over fifty years. This was James, later Sir James, Purves Stewart's *The Diagnosis of Nervous Diseases* originally published at 15s; the tenth edition was published in 1955, at a reasonable 50s. Joe Greener recalled Stewart arriving daily, with his proofs, in his chauffeur-driven car and noted "I seldom saw a more nervous individual".

1908 saw a number of notable books published in various parts of the list. One of the more famous of the memoirs was *The*

Reminiscences of Lady Randolph Churchill, which had a great vogue and reprinted several times in its first two years. An odd feature of this "glittering" book is that Lady Randolph's son Winston makes only seven one-line appearances.

On the school side, there was W. R. Hardie's *Latin Prose Composition* and in the engineering list, F. C. Lea's *Hydraulics*; the former

---

ARNOLD'S
NEW 6s. NOVELS
AUTUMN, 1910

NEW NOVEL by the Author of "A Room with a View."

HOWARD'S END

By E. M. FORSTER

Author of "A Room with a View," "The Longest Journey," etc.

THE RETURN

By
WALTER DE LA MARE

EDWARD ARNOLD
London : 41 & 43 Maddox Street, W.

A typical small leaflet announcing two important new novels. One wonders what Arnold said to the clerk or printer responsible for the intrusive apostrophe in *Howards End*!

remained in print unchanged until the 1960s and the latter's sixth edition until the 1950s.

A pioneering work in the interpretation of eastern art was Laurence Binyon's *Painting in the Far East*, a handsome crown quarto book, including thirty-one collotype plates, and published at one guinea. It became a standard work and the fourth edition, fully revised and published in 1934, remained in print until 1950.

Eleven novels were published, nine of which were fairly run-of-the-mill. One of the other two was Upton Sinclair's *Metropolis*, whose UK edition was probably the result of Arnold's links with New York. The second was introduced in the year's "List of New Books": "A novelist's third book, when its predecessors have shown great promise, is generally held to make or mar his reputation. There can be no question that Mr Forster's new story will effectually establish his position." It did. E. M. Forster's first two novels were published by Blackwood of Edinburgh – *Where Angels Fear to Tread* in 1905 and *The Longest Journey* in 1907. His third novel, *A Room With A View* (originally entitled *Lucy*) came to Arnold no doubt as a result of one of the many letters Arnold wrote to new authors and because he proposed terms to Forster which were more generous than those offered by Blackwood. In 1924 Arnold took over the first two books, when they appeared with others in the uniform edition. After 1908 all of Forster's novels and his principal non-fiction books were published by Arnold and he was looked after by Edward Arnold, then by Brian Fagan and lastly by Anthony Hamilton.

The two volumes of short stories, about which Forster was keen, were refused by Arnold. In 1908, in a letter about other matters, Forster proposed a volume of short stories. Arnold seems to have ignored this part of the letter and, in 1909, when Forster made a firmer proposal, Arnold rejected it on the grounds that there was no public demand for short stories. The first volume was published in 1911 and the second in 1928, both by Sidgwick & Jackson. Arnold was keen to build on the success of *A Room with a View* and urged Forster on to another novel. The first draft manuscript of *Howards End* arrived in March 1910. Forster was grateful for Arnold's criticisms and of them wrote "I feel great

force, and by which I hope to profit". However the Helen se-
duction scene, which worried Arnold, was left in, as Forster felt
it was intrinsic to the plot. *Howards End* was published in October
1910 to critical acclaim, the *Daily Telegraph* acknowledging Forster
now 'as one of the great novelists'. Nothing else significant was
to be published until 1924 but in the meantime Arnold maintained
warm relations with Forster mainly by correspondence. Forster
retained his own copyrights and made all his own arrangements
for US publication and for foreign translations. Arnold gave plenty
of help and advice in these matters but always refused Forster's
offer of agency payments for the work done, for which Forster
was duly grateful. There seem to have been only two points of
difference – one over the royalty of the uniform edition and the
other over the poor printing of *Howards End* in the same edition.
Both were settled amicably. In November 1910 Forster asked
Arnold to clarify an amusing misunderstanding because "It is
rumoured that the Athenaeum announces me as Miss Ethel M.
Forster." Arnold must have done so, as no more was heard of
Ethel.

Between 1901 and 1910 Arnold published about 760 titles –
reaching a new peak with 104 books in 1910. The balance of the
list was very similar to the first ten years, there being over 330
schoolbooks. On the general side there were ninety new novels;
biography and travel were the next largest sections. By now
medicine had become more significant, with thirty titles, and
nursing was just emerging with one title. In 1910 itself, apart from
Howards End, Arnold published another novel by a rising literary
figure, *The Return* by Walter de la Mare, whose reputation was
not to come from his novels. Also published in 1910 was a further
plea for the reform of British Army thinking, Erskine Childers's
War and the Arme Blanche (to be followed in 1911 by his *German
Influence on British Cavalry*).

In 1909 Arnold spotted some stories and articles in *The Teacher's
World* written by a young elementary schoolteacher, C. S. Evans,
and took him on as educational editor. Evans left in 1913, invited
by William Heinemann to help start an educational list. In fact he
quickly moved over to the general side, was Chairman from 1929
to 1944, and was described by the *Manchester Guardian* as "one of

THE

WALLET

SERIES

OF

HANDBOOKS

PRICE PER VOLUME
Paper Covers, 1s. net; post free, 1s. 2d.
Cloth, 2s. net; post free, 2s. 2d.
Size, Fcap. 8vo.

A forerunner of many pocket-book series. *The Wallet Series* prospered from 1900–1919 and was available in cloth at 2s and paper at 1s. It ranged from the practical to the artistic, with such titles as: *Dress Outfits for Abroad, On Collecting Miniatures, Enamels and Jewellery* and *Electric Lighting For The Inexperienced* the most influential publishers of our time". At Arnold's he was responsible for several successful schoolbooks and his own book, *Nash and Some Others*, a collection of wryly observed and amusing stories of schoolboys, was published by Arnold in 1913.

In 1911 Arnold started a new series, *International Medical Monographs* under the editorship of Leonard, later Sir Leonard, Hill. Many volumes were published over the next few years, covering such diverse topics as digestion, nutrition, caisson sickness and syphilis. The first secretarial books were published in this year as *Arnold's Secretarial Studies*, dealing with touch typewriting and accounts. This is another area where the company has continued to publish up to the present day – not very extensively, but reputably and profitably.

The religious list, so far comfortable and "establishment", had an addition in 1911 which caused consternation in some quarters. The Reverend J. M. Thompson was a "modernist" Fellow of Magdalen College Oxford and in his book, *Miracles in the New Testament*, he argued that the miraculous elements were not historically trustworthy, and could be surrendered without prejudice to Christianity. He was fiercely attacked, his licence was withdrawn by one Bishop and he was inhibited by another. One orthodox bookseller told the Arnold representative, "If you leave that hateful book on the pavement outside, I will look at the others". Thompson wrote a second book in 1913, *Through Facts to Faith*, in which he attempted further to show that Christian faith is strengthened by accepting the conclusions of historical and scientific criticism. The controversy still comes alive from time to time.

Another book that year which had far-reaching implications was Erskine Childers' *The Framework of Home Rule*. There are many who think that, if the policies in this well-reasoned book had been followed, the situation in Ireland would be very different today.

As we have seen, Arnold had already published a number of books by eminent people on the need to prepare militarily and politically for a quickly changing world. In 1912 he published a translation of *Germany and the Next War* by General F. von Bernhardi, which was "to turn a staid publisher's office into a good imitation of an evening newspaper's distribution department on Derby Day". Typical of the reviews were *The Spectator*: "This singular book is a very wholesome study for English readers.

General von Bernhardi asserts plainly and repeatedly that war between Britain and Germany is inevitable"; and *The Pall Mall Gazette*: "In England soldiers, sailors, newspapers have preached to the people – and to the politicians – the inevitability of such a war; and in the main such preaching has fallen on deaf ears". It was difficult to keep the book in stock and the demand increased geometrically up to August 1914. The first edition was published in October 1912 at 10s 6d and was reprinted immediately and throughout 1913. In 1914 a "New Popular Edition" was published in paper at 2s, followed one month later by a "Popular Edition" in cloth at 2s 6d. The book remained in print until after the Second World War – presumably for historians.

Other aspects of the list were not neglected in 1912, when Arnold published the first two volumes of Oliver Elton's *A Survey of English Literature, 1780–1830*. Elton had succeeded Raleigh as professor of English Literature at Liverpool University. His next two volumes, covering *1830–1880*, were published in 1920 and the last two, dealing with *1730–1780*, appeared in 1928. D. Nichol Smith described these six books as ". . . the fullest account that any single writer has attempted of any 150 years of our literature. Their value lies in the sanity and freshness of the estimates of individual authors or works". The six books remained in print until the early 1960s and anyone reading them today would still agree with Nichol Smith's assessment. In 1912 Arnold published a total of 130 books – the largest number which the company was to produce while Edward Arnold was a partner; they covered the whole range of his publishing and included nearly fifty schoolbooks.

In the year before "the Great War" output fell to ninety-eight books, of which half were for schools. Two further books by Harry Graham were published and also a first novel by Leonard Woolf, *The Village in the Jungle*. The book, based on Woolf's colonial service experience in Ceylon, was a sympathetic study of rural life there. Forster was delighted with it – even though it seems Arnold had required some cutting of the more delicate passages! Woolf's second and last novel was published in 1914. *The Wise Virgins* portrayed a totally different scene in a story concerned with a very artistic and intellectual London circle on the one hand, and an unsophisticated surburban family on the other.

Both books remained in print until the 1930s. Other notable and longer-lived books came from other parts of the list. The first edition of *Diseases of Children*, edited by Archibald, later Sir Archibald, Garrod and F. E. Batten, was an important and a large work. It contained 1200 pages, was heavily illustrated and was published at 30s. Over the years new editions were published and new editors joined the panel. The Fifth Edition, published in 1956 at £7, lasted until the early 70s. Another very successful book was R. W. Willows's *Textbook of Physics* written for sixth forms and first year university students. It had three editions and a life of fifty years. It was particularly successful in India, where several thousand copies were sold each year.

In 1914 life became more difficult for the country and for Edward Arnold. A number of the staff, including Joe Greener, were in the Territorial Army and were quickly drafted – others went later. Arnold promised all members of staff who joined the services that he would find them a job after the war – "even if it was window-cleaning". He kept his promise without resort to the windows. Output dropped to fifty-one titles in 1914; one of these was a technical book, Adam and Evans *Metalwork*, which retained its supremacy in its field for thirty years and lasted for a further twenty years as a reasonable seller. The difficulties of the war years are of course reflected in Arnold's publishing programme: 1915 saw forty-five books published, in 1916 the number fell to twenty-eight, in 1917 there were twenty-nine and in 1918, sixteen, the lowest figure since 1890. During these years such books that were published continued to reflect Arnold's interests. One of the sporting books sits oddly with the others, namely *Thirty Years a Boxing Referee* by Eugene Corri (1915), but at least it had an aristocratic Foreword by the Earl of Lonsdale. The fiction list faltered, dropping to one title in 1916, back to nine in 1917 and none in 1918. Arnold showed a good publisher's awareness of the war and its implications and published about thirty books on various aspects of the war. Some were to deal with immediate and eye-witness accounts, such as *The Zeppelin Raid in West Norfolk* by H. Ingleby (1915) and *A Surgeon in Belgium*, which covered the period from September 1914 to March 1915 and was swiftly published in April 1915. Others were books professional in nature, looking to future needs, such as Arthur, later Sir Arthur, Hurst's

Medical Diseases of War, 1917 and S. F. Card's *Air Navigation, Notes and Examples*, 1919. He also attempted to get authoritative books on particular campaigns or spheres; sometimes he succeeded, as with C. C. Turner's *Struggle in the Air* and sometimes he failed, as with Lord Jellicoe in 1916 and Lord Allenby in 1918/19.

In March 1916 Arnold suffered a tragic personal loss. He wrote to John Murray explaining that one of his daughters, Peggy, had been nursing in France for nine months when suddenly he heard that she had died after only two days' illness. He wrote: "It is a terrible and overwhelming blow, for she was everything that one could wish a daughter to be, but we are very proud of her having died 'on active service' and I like to think that she was able to alleviate many a poor fellow's suffering". Later in the year Arnold published for private circulation *Peggy's Diary at No. 16 General Hospital*; it was a cheerful yet moving account of a war-time hospital under canvas and in the mud. Peggy comes through the pages as a bright, caring and sensitive young woman, suddenly thrust into acute discomfort and suffering.

In 1917 a medical classic was published, *Midwifery* by Ten Teachers under the direction of Comyns, later Sir Comyns, Berkeley. The contributors were all distinguished members of the London teaching hospitals. The price was 18s then. Now in its fourteenth edition under the title of *Obstetrics by Ten Teachers*, it continues to be the standard text, selling at £14.95.

It is interesting to note that the war even had its effect on the schoolbooks then being published, for example two readers: *Les Français en Guerre* (1915) and *Sur le Front* (1916).

Although 1918 was the least active for new books, it was also the year when Arnold started his school music list. Thomas F. Dunhill had married Arnold's daughter Mary in 1914. A composer of note, he was a professor at the Royal College of Music and acted as Arnold's music editor. In June 1918 the first fifty pieces of *Singing Class Music* were published at 3d. or 4d. each. The words were taken from a variety of sources and the music was written by a wide range of composers including such names as Dunhill himself, Howells, Parry, Holst, Dyson, Stanford, Wood and Ireland. The *Singing Class Music* list prospered and by 1940 there were over 450 songs available, some fifty descants, thirty pianoforte pieces, song books and operettas. The whole list was sold in 1959 to Novello, where it continues. Robin Dunhill was told by his father Thomas that E.A. had asked him to join the firm as a partner to develop the music publishing side of the business. However Mary would not countenance this "saying that she had married a composer, not a businessman!"

4

1919–1930

OUTPUT increased in 1919 to thirty-six books, of which nine were related to the War. There was no fiction other than M. R. James's *A Thin Ghost*. There was, however, another of the medical classics, *Diseases of Women* by Ten Teachers under the direction of Comyns Berkeley. Originally published at 30s, it is now in its fourteenth edition under the title of *Gynaecology by Ten Teachers*, published at £14.95.

In 1919 several members of the staff returned to the company from military or other service and new members joined. Among the former were F. P. (Fred) Dunn and H. J. D. (Joe) Greener. Dunn, a chemist by training, had joined Arnold before the war as science editor. During the war he had worked for the Government on the problems presented by poison gas. Throughout his life he was closely associated with Balham Congregational Church and was for many years the Superintendent of the Sunday School, which, at its peak, had about 1000 students, one of whom was the footballer and commentator Jimmy Hill. The Sunday School also provided a good source for recruiting many young people to the Arnold staff, including John Chandler, who joined the warehouse before the Second World War, after which he became foreman and gave fifty years service to the company.

During the twenties and thirties Dunn was responsible for a fine list of science books, including research monographs and textbooks. On the research side he published such significant books as F. W. Aston's *Isotopes* (1922), an integral part of the Cambridge work on nuclear energy, and M. W. Travers's *The Discovery of the Rare Gases*. Probably Dunn's most famous textbooks were those by the great chemistry teacher E. J. Holmyard, Head of Science at

Clifton College. His four books for schools and colleges, published between 1922 and 1930, set a new pattern of chemistry teaching; they became the standard works for twenty years and went on selling for a further twenty.

Joe Greener returned to the Education department and shortly took on the role of educational representative. At different periods he covered the whole country and his knowledge of schools, staff and syllabuses was encyclopaedic. He went on working, especially training new overseas agents, after his retirement in 1962. He was judged to be, by his own company and all his competitors, one of the truly great "reps". His value to Arnold was enormous as, so often, it was Joe's first intelligence which sent John Morgan and then Bryan Bennett off to recruit authors like E. W. Young, G. Richardson, Michael Davies and Alan Shaw.

Captain B. W. Fagan of the Ox and Bucks Light Infantry had been badly wounded in the war. Before the war he had been Head Boy at Rugby and went on to Queen's College, Oxford, where he took a first in Mods, but before completing his degree he joined the Army. Had it not been for the war and his wounds, he would probably have followed his father, Sir Patrick Fagan, and made a career in the Indian Civil Service. As it was, he joined Edward Arnold as head of the Education department. Both he and F. P. Dunn became partners in the company in 1921. Brian Fagan seemed to disregard his artificial leg; he cycled to the office, drove a motor car and also played tennis. He started immediately to call on public schools (the first naturally being Rugby) and universities and, with leads from Edward Arnold, started looking for authors. He also visited the better grammar schools but, unlike Arnold, his interests did not extend to the elementary or primary sectors of education. He was musical and gradually took over the running of the Arnold school music department. During the twenties Fagan published a number of books for public and grammar schools, the most successful of which were the five textbooks and five exercise books which made up C. B. Thurston's *A Progressive Geography*. This series became the standard course through the late twenties and the thirties and remained in print until after the Second World War. He was also responsible for a number of English books by Guy Boas, including the *Touchstone Shakespeare*, a series of twelve edited plays which had a successful life of some twenty-five years.

During the twenties Fagan was also responsible for a number of distinguished university and scholarly books in English, such as W. L. Renwick *Edmund Spenser* and W. Macneile Dixon *Tragedy*, and more particularly in history, for example J. Huizinga *The Waning of the Middle Ages*, W. W. Tarn *Hellenistic Civilisation* and a number of books on European and US diplomacy by R. B. Mowat.

At this point, after Edward Arnold had been building his list successfully and mainly on his own for thirty years, it is interesting to look back at some of "the ones that got away". Few records remain from before 1900, but in the early years of the new century Arnold pursued the eminent and the "up-and-coming" to write on politics, history, exploration and literature. Lord Curzon in 1901 explained that he had no leisure and that in any event "a Viceroy should be above writing". Lord Wolseley was flattered but wrote "I am not supposed to give any public expression to my views which are far in advance of those who are my superiors". In 1906 Baden-Powell apologized to Arnold for having fallen "victim to the persuasive powers of Smith & Elder to write a book on Africa"; but he hoped that he "may get another chance in future of working with you". Admiral of the Fleet Lord Fisher (or his secretary) wrote briefly in 1910 "that he was obliged to Mr Arnold but does not contemplate doing anything at present" (but he later wrote for Hodder & Stoughton). An approach to Winston Churchill in 1905 brought a typically opportunistic reply: "I am carefully considering it in conjunction with other offers and suggestions I have received".

In 1902 J. M. Barrie thanked Arnold "heartily" for his letter, "but at present I do not propose to publish my plays". A more orotund G. K. Chesterton answered "a very complimentary suggestion" put in 1904 that he should prepare a book on Christian controversy with the fear that such a work could not appear until after other books he had promised. Joseph Conrad wrote from Italy in 1905 with a portrait which all aspiring authors might profit from. "I am one of those authors who write at a desk whose drawers are empty and by the side of a waste paper basket which foams full, overbrim, with torn up pages . . . Every child of the Earth has the right to be afraid of something – and I own to a dread of twaddle, morbid (perhaps) but less unhealthy (perhaps) than the self-confidence which welcomes every plausible thought, every facile expression." In other words, he "had nothing ready for immediate publication".

A. C. Bradley, Gilbert Murray and G. M. Trevelyan were examples of those who were already committed elsewhere and T. E. Lawrence one who was not yet ready. In 1919, probably at E. M. Forster's suggestion, Arnold wrote twice to Lawrence, who refused the offer of publication saying ". . . since my narrative of the Arab affair is very detailed, and far <u>too private</u> to admit of publication at the present time – and till this is finished to my entire satisfaction (years hence) I cannot write anything else". [*The Seven Pillars of Wisdom* was finally printed for private circulation in 1926.] The list gives some idea of Arnold's awareness and industry over the years and also shows that then, as now, "you can't win 'em all".

During these same years it is unlikely that the appearance or the atmosphere of the offices in Maddox Street changed very much. From reminiscences by Joe Greener [1912–66], Paul Edmonds [1926–46 in production and publicity, subsequently Managing Director of Cleaver–Hume], Mervyn Mills [1924–27 as general assistant, now historian and playwright] and Laurie Vogel [1929–80 in the Trade Department, Manager for twenty-four years] it is possible to visualize it in the period just before the First World War until the late 1920s. Handsome brass-plated swing doors opened from the street onto the main office, where there was absolute quiet except for the ticking of the clock over the fireplace. Two rows of Dickensian high desks faced each other, complete with brass rails to hold the invoice books and ledgers. Originally those sitting on the stools were all male, but gradually one or two ladies were employed, who were always dressed in neat green overalls. There was only one telephone originally and that was in the main office, to which even Mr Arnold would have to be summoned by some primitive internal dialling mechanism. To the left of the office was the reception area, where even very distinguished visitors had to wait the statutory few minutes for the "great man" to see them.

In the corner of the main office was a glazed smaller office inhabited by the General Manager Mr T. Walford, a large, portly Oxford man who dominated the rather short Edward Arnold – in size only! Arnold was neat and pink, somewhat peppery in speech and given to asking further questions before earlier ones had been answered. To the right of the main office and in its own section opening onto the road was the Trade Department. Here members of that departed species, the Collectors, would gather bringing the latest gossip from the trade. Larger parcels for depots and the Post Office would emerge in the street on the hydraulic lift from the basement for loading into Mr Moxon's horse van. The basement, where the stock was kept and packed, was ruled by Mr Clare, an RSM-like figure, whom all the office staff remembered to call Mister – "a wonderful larger-than-life character, who held sway downstairs and who, with his massive arms folded across his brawny chest, would tell dramatic stories of London Life". He was also the caretaker, his wife the housekeeper, and they lived in the flat at the top of 41/43. It was there that their son Tom was born, who was later to play such an important part in the development of the company and who was to become its Chairman in 1962.

On the first floor, apart from Edward Arnold, there were four other rooms, occupied by A. L. Mumm, Harry Graham and other senior editors. One of these was W. E. Candy, who was the education editor for some years and who even made trips to Australasia and Hong Kong. He left the company in 1920 to look after Longman's Indian branches, and could be called the founder of the Longman ELT empire, as he was the sponsor of Michael West's *New Method Readers*. Sadly, he was drowned in 1941, when his ship was torpedoed in the Indian Ocean.

The second floor was inhabited by lesser editors, and publicity clerks and eventually one, then two secretaries, who were dressed in seemly black. Before their arrival all letters were hand-written, pressed in a copying machine, dried and then kept in leather-bound copy books, alas now all lost.

On the production side we have seen that Arnold, certainly in the early years, did much himself. Later, about 1905, he appointed D. C. Walford to be in charge of "blocks" and advertising. As far as one can tell, "being in charge of blocks" principally meant that, wherever possible, half tone illustrations should be used more than once and that making the blocks should be so organized that as

Trade Only. **1913.**

SPECIAL OFFER FOR LENT.

We shall have pleasure in invoicing a Stock Order, received on or before February 12th, for any of the following net publications **at one-third off the published prices** net, no odds.

EDWARD ARNOLD.

ORDER FORM.

To MR. EDWARD ARNOLD,

41 & 43, MADDOX STREET,

LONDON, W.

Please send by..

Name..

Address..

Date................................1913................................

THEOLOGICAL WORKS.

JESUS SALVATOR MUNDI. By **Rev. J. H. Beibitz**	**2/6** *net*
THE CROWN OF THORNS. By **Rev. A. E. Burn**	**2/6** *net*
THE SAINTS' APPEAL. By **Rev. Canon S. A. Alexander**	**2/-** *net*
THROUGH FACTS TO FAITH. By **Rev. J. M. Thompson**	**3/6** *net*
MIRACLES OF THE NEW TESTAMENT. By **Rev. J. M. Thompson**	**3/6** *net*

The first page of a special leaflet, which "allied piety with profit".

49

many as possible should be made together to the same reduction, thus saving several pence. The large guard books in which block pulls were pasted remained in the main office. As the few ladies employed by the firm passed by these books, chivalry dictated that those pages containing the medical illustrations should be lightly gummed shut. Book design seems to have been done largely by the printers on general lines indicated by Arnold or the editors.

There appears to have been little promotion to the trade – other than *Mr Edward Arnold's Trade Catalogue*, which came out yearly. Into each catalogue would also be bound the New Book Announcements of usually sixteen pages, the Catalogue of Standard and General Literature, broken into subjects ranging from "Books For The Country-House" down to "Miscellaneous", usually twenty-four pages and, finally, the General Educational Catalogue, again by subject and numbering forty-eight pages. Other than "removal" offers, there remains one other example of a special offer to the trade, which may or may not have been a regular practice. In 1913 Mr Edward Arnold allied piety with profit by his 'Special Offer for Lent', whereby booksellers who placed stock orders before 12 February of some forty-seven theological works, ranging from 2s to 12s 6d, were offered "one third off the published prices net, no odds".

Advertisements were placed in the press but these were of the "reader-ad" variety without vulgar display. In the early 1900s Arnold issued his announcements in two-colour quarto booklets sometimes as *"Attractive New Books"* or *"New and Popular Books"* or just *"New Books"*. These would include forbidding posed photographs of some authors and the occasional photograph from a mountaineering or travel book.

As well as catalogues, Arnold also had printed a variety of leaflets in a variety of sizes, but usually a single leaf. Such leaflets might advertise just one book or sometimes half a dozen related titles. These pieces were placed inside the books, sometimes by the binder and sometimes in house. The copy for these promotional pieces was often still written by Arnold himself until the mid 1920s, when Paul Edmonds arrived to take charge of advertising and publicity. Until the 1920s all general books except the largest and most sumptuous had bound in at the back the new Announce-

RECENT & STANDARD NOVELS

Published by EDWARD ARNOLD & CO.

E. M. FORSTER	A Passage to India
ANNE DOUGLAS SEDGWICK	Adrienne Toner
GEORGE A. BIRMINGHAM	The Seething Pot
M. E. COLERIDGE	The King with Two Faces
DOROTHEA CONYERS	The Boy, Some Horses, and a Girl
DOROTHEA CONYERS	Peter's Pedigree
OSWALD H. DAVIS	Soft Goods
J. M. FALKNER	Moonfleet
E. M. FORSTER	Howards End
E. M. FORSTER	A Room with a View
L. C. HOBART	The Silken Scarf
ARTHUR HOUGHAM	Gabriel Quelford
M. R. JAMES	Ghost Stories of an Antiquary
WILLIAM McFEE	Aliens
F. F. MONTRÉSOR	The Celestial Surgeon
J. CRANSTOUN NEVILL	The Gates are Open
FORREST REID	Following Darkness
FORREST REID	The Gentle Lover
FORREST REID	The Spring Song
MRS. ALFRED SEDGWICK	The Beryl Stones
MARY J. H. SKRINE	The Black Cow
GERTRUDE SPINNY	The Painted Castle
F. T. WAWN	Jacynth

EDWARD ARNOLD & CO.
LONDON : 41 & 43 MADDOX STREET, W1

A list of Arnold's leading novelists in 1924.

ments, ranging from eight to thirty-two pages in extent. Also placed in books as they were despatched was a postcard which invited customers to indicate their interests. Mailing lists were thus built up for future announcements; these lists were numbered more in hundreds than in thousands.

Although there were two or three travellers, including the legendary Harry Clifford, there was no sales manager; once a week it was a clerk from the trade department or publicity who would take to Arnold, precisely at 12 noon, the tally of the week's orders from Mudies, Harrods, Days, Smiths, Boots and Simpkins. Nothing else need be done because it was felt that the Arnold name was respected in the Trade as a publisher of good books which would sell themselves.

In 1920 Edward Arnold was 63 and having built his house, Pook Hill at Chiddingford, Surrey, came to the office only four days a week. He changed trains at Guildford and was looked after by a particular porter, who asked if there might be an opening for his son. Arnold interviewed young John Carter on the station and offered him a job as clerk. John Carter later became a representative, moved to Putnam's in the late 20s, became sales manager of Routledge, Kegan and Paul in 1935, then a director and finally Chairman in 1961.

Although Arnold was not so active, he was still responsible for a number of books each year until 1930. Little fiction was published except between 1923 and 1928, when the number of titles ranged from five to ten a year and included such popular authors as Anne Sedgwick and Mary Skrine; no fiction was published in 1930. Forster finally produced another novel, *A Passage to India*, which was published in 1924 to immediate critical acclaim. It also created some unease and hostility among the more right-wing imperialists – a typical comment, from a relative of Lord Lugard's, was "Horrid! The man's a bounder." The first printing in May was 5000 copies. It then reprinted five times during the year, totalling 20,000 copies. Arnold took this opportunity to take over publication of Forster's first two novels, *Where Angels Fear to Tread* and *The Longest Journey*, which, together with *A Room With A View* and *Howards End*, were all issued in the Uniform Edition at 5s each. *A Passage to India* was put into the same edition in 1926. In 1927 Arnold published *Aspects of the Novel*, which was based on the Clark Lectures given by Forster in Cambridge earlier in the year. After dealing personally and happily with Forster for over twenty years, it seems odd that Arnold, when he was retiring, did not himself tell Forster but left it to Brian Fagan to write. Forster expressed his surprise and said that he would write to Arnold, and went on to say; "I am sure that the pleasant relationships I have had with the firm will be continued under yourself and Mr Dunn". Apart from fiction, Arnold continued to publish books of reminiscences, sporting and travel books and works of criticism up to his retirement in December 1930.

Mumm made occasional appearances until 1926, when he withdrew from the partnership. However his Alpine links remained valuable and gave rise to four remarkable books. The first was *Mount Everest, The Reconnaissance* by Colonel C. R. Howard-Bury, published in 1922, which included an account of the delicate diplomacy needed to obtain permission from the Governments of India and Tibet. This was followed in 1923 by *The Assault on Mount Everest* by the leader of the 1922 expedition, Brigadier-General C. G. Bruce. The third book, published in 1925, told the most dramatic story of the 1924 expedition. Written by Colonel E. F. Norton, the expedition leader, and other members of the expedition, *The Fight for Everest* shows a photograph of Norton at 28100 feet – the highest point ever climbed – and leaves unanswered the great question: Did Mallory and Irvine reach the summit? The whole story of these expeditions was retold by Sir Francis Younghusband in his classic book *The Epic of Everest* published in 1926. It is fitting that this magnificent Everest story should find its conclusion in *Ascent of Everest*, published in 1953 by Hodder & Stoughton, of which Edward Arnold now forms a part.

During the 1920s Fagan and Dunn began to discover their own new authors. On the school side the company did not benefit, as other publishers did, from the great expansion in the senior elementary schools following H. A. L. Fisher's 1918 Education Act, but it continued to add new titles for grammar and public schools in English, modern languages, history and geography. From 1925 to 1930 there were about twenty such titles published per year.

The school music list grew considerably in the 1920s and, during the ten years, about 180 pieces for class singing and choirs, forty

Colonel Norton at 28000 feet. In 1924 this was the highest that man
had climbed and the highest point at which photographs had been
taken. (From *The Epic of Mount Everest*)

pieces for the piano and five song books were published under the general editorship of Thomas Dunhill.

Nearly sixty medical books, including new editions, appeared during the decade, split evenly between texts and monographs. Most of them had useful long lives, but two stand out as of lasting significance to the company and to the medical world. The first was *Textbook of Pathology*, written by Robert Muir, Professor of Pathology at the University of Glasgow, and published in 1924. The second edition was published in 1929 and now, in its twelfth edition, it continues to share the world market in English and translations with its main American competitors. The other book arose from an invitation by Arnold to the Professor and the Reader in Bacteriology at the London School of Hygiene for a book to cover the needs of postgraduate medical students. *The Principles of Bacteriology and Immunology*, immediately dubbed "Topley and Wilson", was published in two volumes at 50s in 1929. It became the most internationally distinguished work in its field, which it remains now in its eighth edition published in 1990 in five volumes at £395.

By the end of 1930, when Arnold retired, the company had 1500 titles in print, of which about 600 were school books. Apart from running his own firm, Arnold had, over the years, taken an active part in trade affairs. It was in Arnold's room that the first meeting of the Education Group of Publishers was held in 1917. He served on the PA Council and several of its committees, including that which met the Governers of the BBC to clarify the fields in which it should publish books. In 1928/29 Arnold took over the Presidency of the PA from W. M. Meredith, whose health was failing.

In the middle of 1930 Edward Arnold came to the office in a "rather merry mood" and announced to the staff in the main office that he was "embarking upon a new adventure" – namely that he was to be married again; his wife Minnie had died some years previously. His second wife, Christina Burland, was considerably younger than he was and the *Daily Mirror* reported the event with a picture of the happy couple over the caption "Aged publisher weds". When Arnold retired in December 1930, they moved to Budleigh Salterton, where they led a very happy life until Arnold died on 6 November 1942, at the age of 85. In his obituary in the

Bookseller, Brian Fagan described Arnold as "a successful publisher of the old grand and courteous school". Fagan went on to ask why Arnold "had never developed a catalogue comparable in size with those of some firms who were his contemporaries or even his juniors". He gave two answers: first, although Arnold knew how to take risks, he "also had an instinct of cautious moderation unsympathetic, for instance, to strongly competitive methods of expansion"; second, "publishing was not merely his business, but his prime interest . . . a publisher should not only be continuously familiar with every detail of his own organisation, but also should not publish more books than the number which he, like a faithful midwife-cum-monthly-nurse could treat as living entities". Looking back on this verdict nearly fifty years on, not only do we see the value of it but we would add that no other single publisher of his generation created such a wide list, in each part of which were books of great worth and so often of a very long life. In his forty years Arnold had laid the foundation of a company, known and respected internationally, which survived as an independent for almost ninety-eight years, long after most of his contemporaries had been absorbed into other organizations.

In 1912 *T. P.'s Weekly* had described Edward Arnold thus: "By recreation he is a fisherman, a lover of the open air; by profession a literary man, whose gift is that of selection". Having selected his authors over a wide field, Arnold seems to have looked after them rather well – and often over periods of twenty years or so, as we have seen in the case of Viscount Milner, Sir Walter Raleigh and E. M. Forster. As always in the business of publishing, there were rumours that Arnold could be "careful" over the question of royalties, but there is no evidence to support this. On the contrary, many of his agreements with novelists, including E. M. Forster, were made on the basis of royalties as high as 25 per cent on all copies sold. Where, as he did in his early years, he bought the copyright of a book, a typical fee was £1000, which was not ungenerous and could lead to a loss. For general and scholarly books, the royalty usually started at 10 per cent and rose to 15 per cent after 500 or 1000 copies, terms then considered very reasonable. Arnold also, as we have seen, often looked after his authors' wider interests, particularly in relation to American editions and various translations involving much work for no financial reward.

It is not surprising, therefore, that nearly all his authors stayed loyal to Arnold. Apart from those already mentioned, they included Sir Ian Hamilton (four books), Sir Herbert Maxwell (ten), Anne Douglas Sedgwick (six), Mary Skrine (six) and many more. It is illuminating to take just two examples of how his authors viewed Edward Arnold, never himself a demonstrative man. First, in 1908, Anne Douglas Sedgwick was writing to him about an alternative proposal she had received: ". . . it would require a very large inducement indeed to make me abandon the prospect of a publisher so appreciative as yourself". Much later, in 1924, Viola Meynell, thanking Arnold for his most kind letter, wrote: "How much I hope there may be some success to reward you for the encouragement and appreciation you have so generously given me. No one could have a more perfect publisher". One of the few people who remember Arnold personally is his grandson David Dunhill, who describes him at three periods in his life. First when the grandson was a young boy in the 1920s and Arnold was still working. After playing or reading with their grandmother, the grandchildren would go to the study to say goodnight to their grandfather. They knocked nervously and went into the book-lined room to receive a good night kiss. David Dunhill writes: "I think we were all rather frightened of him – and that included our parents. He wasn't physically frightening: he was a very small man. The main dread was of appearing to be in some way bad-mannered". Later, about 1930, he continues: "In adolescence I continued to be nervous in his presence although I rarely had need to be. He changed into a dinner jacket each evening and as soon as my brother and I were old enough (fifteen, perhaps, in my case) we were expected to 'dress for dinner' too, when we were staying in his house.

A little ritual was performed outside the front door of 'Pook' before we went back to school at the beginning of each term. Grandpa hovered about near the door of the car and we hovered just as awkwardly, awaiting the inevitable 'tip' and trying hard not to look as though we were expecting it. The coin, a half-crown, perhaps, was pressed into a palm with all the pretended nonchalance of handing a tip to the head waiter.

After his second marriage, Grandpa softened greatly. I began to see him as a human being and to appreciate – even sometimes to want to emulate – the courteous, kindly qualities embodied in this member of a generation twice removed from mine. He even made me feel he was fond of me."

5

1930–1945

THE retirement of Edward Arnold in 1930 was a watershed in the history of the firm, and it is worthwhile to look at this in some detail, as far as the remaining records allow.

Arnold's retirement was preceded, in 1926, by that of A. L. Mumm, his partner of many years. Mumm's investment in the partnership, of £7000, was repaid to him in October, 1926; he also received a goodwill payment of £3742, based on four eighteenths of the profits averaged over three years after deduction of interest. The relevant profits, for 1923, 1924 and 1925 were £16723, £19295 and £19750 respectively – a very steady performance. Mumm also had an interest in the Maddox Street building which were owned personally by Arnold, and later left to his wife: these were leased to the partners for £1500 per annum.

When it came to Edward Arnold's own retirement, Brian Fagan and Fred Dunn were required to find the then very hefty sum of £43981.11.9 in order to take over the partnership. This was made up of £24750 capital plus £19231.11.9 goodwill. Of this total sum the two younger partners had by 1930 already repaid £10995.7.11 out of their share of the profits, leaving a balance of £32986.3.10. It was arranged that this sum should be paid to Arnold in three further instalments of £10955.7.11, (plus interest at 5 per cent) in December 1931, June 1932 and December 1932.

It was obvious that sums of this kind – perhaps three six-monthly payments of £150 000 at today's values – could not be produced by the two partners out of their own pockets. They therefore approached Coutts, in the person of Eric Carpenter, who was then working in the loan department; he will appear again later in this book. The bank agreed to provide £16000 (later increased) by way of an overdraft, so that interest was payable only when the money was being used. The security provided was the lease on the Maddox Street building and an insurance policy taken out by the two partners on each other's life for £15000.

This arrangement with the bank made it possible for Fagan and Dunn to proceed with the purchase, but they had a hard struggle for several years, especially as the payments had to be made at the start of the great slump. Early in the 1930s one or two staff cuts had to be made, and the whole staff had their salaries temporarily reduced by ten per cent. In May, 1932 Fagan wrote to Arnold saying that the depression was making life very difficult, and that he and Dunn were not confident of being able to make the final payment at the end of the year; this would depend on how well the autumn school book sales survived the coming cuts. Familiar feelings! Arnold replied to this information coolly but civilly. In the event, the final repayment to Arnold was made on time; but the partners were not able to clear their indebtedness to Coutts until October 1937.

The terms imposed by Edward Arnold were always remembered by his successors as being harsh. The writer remembers an occasion in the 1950s when, for the first time, a very modest showroom had been established in Maddox Street; a fairly comprehensive display of books was provided, as well as a table, chairs and a rug. It was suggested that this would be suitably embellished by a portrait of the founder. This proposal was duly referred to the Board, and duly rejected. However, a very attractive consequence of this feeling of having been harshly treated was to be found in Fagan's and Dunn's extremely generous behaviour when their own turn came to retire. It is scarcely desirable to make a judgement at this distance, but one cannot help feeling that, although Arnold's terms were tough, it was not unnatural for him to want a full price for the firm that he alone had created, and worked so hard and so successfully to develop.

There can be no doubt that Fagan and Dunn had a very tough time in the thirties. It was their efforts that ensured the survival of the firm. Life was austere: the partners were often to be seen having a one shilling lunch at J. Lyons in Bond Street, and playing draughts borrowed from the cashier. Fagan, on becoming Senior Partner, decided that he should take on the general list, which had, of course, been Arnold's responsibility; and as a consequence of this he gave up the school books. He published a considerable number of distinguished books, as will be seen; but it seems that he and Dunn, faced with tight funds and a very difficult market, agreed to concentrate on doing what was least risky, and the result of this was that, in publishing terms, the thirties was Dunn's decade.

A perusal of the trade catalogues of that period is a rewarding occupation. Some important information, such as length and date of publication, is absent; but each book had to have its own code for purposes of telegraphic ordering, and this meant that the trade department staff had the right and the duty to provide a nickname for every book published. Some of these were mildly witty in an affectionate sort of way: Brian Hone's *Cricket Practice and Tactics*, for example, was baptised HOOK. But one has the feeling that Harry Graham cannot have been universally loved by the staff on discovering that three of his books were coded GROIN, GRUNT and GUANO. More importantly, a comparison of the list of 1938 with that of 1930 reveals some clear trends in the publishing. In outline, science was very strong, the general publishing less prolific, but containing some excellent books; but the school book and medical publishing were relatively weak. Why was this?

On the school books front, two editors were appointed early on in the period: J. A. Brendon had been a fairly successful author (*The Building of the Modern World*), and Philip Magnus was later, as Sir Philip Magnus-Allcroft, to become one, but, for whatever reason, neither succeeded at Edward Arnold. In 1934 John Morgan was appointed; he was 23, and had been with John Murray for eighteen months, where he was spotted by Joe Greener. He travelled widely among schools of all kinds, and made many contacts which were to prove valuable later, notably Margaret Elliott (*We are their Heirs*) and M. M. Reese (*The Tudors and Stuarts* and many other books); but his career was shortly to be interrupted by the war, and relatively few books came out from him before 1939.

Tom Clare, a few years older than John, had made a solid start in publishing for the technical and commercial schools, both areas which were to remain important to the firm. Many of the books which Tom published during the thirties were familiar to members of staff as important sellers throughout the fifties and sixties.

Boothroyd: *Applied Mechanics* (1931) and Moorfield and Winstanley: *Mechanics and Applied Heat* (1932) are two good technical examples, as is Roberts: *Elementary Bookkeeping Exercises* on the commercial side; but probably the most impressive of all was Jones: *Groundwork of Commerce*. This two-volume text, first published in 1935, has sold continuously since that date in editions first revised by the author, H. L. Jones, and later by his son, R. P. Jones. R. P. Jones was recruited by Bryan Bennett as part of the drive to expand the commerce list. At that time Jones was a bank manager, but he was interested in education and became a lecturer and later Head of Department in Highbury Technical College. These famous books went on through many editions (the seventh was published in 1984), including several specially adapted for West Africa.

Tom Clare did not start his connection with the medical list until the middle thirties and few new medical books were published during this time, though the grand old titles were carefully revised when necessary. In 1935 Tom made a breakthrough with Gordon Sears's *Medicine for Nurses*, the first of several books by this author which were to be of very great importance to the firm, and leading contenders in the marketplace. Tom also pursued his interest in what might be called lower level medical publishing with some other successful titles, such as Galloway's *Anatomy and Physiology of Physical Training* (1938).

In 1930 F. P. Dunn was in his mid-forties, and the pre-war decade saw the apogee of his publishing. He produced a large number of scientific books in various disciplines and at various levels, most of them long-lived, and some of them still in the catalogue more than fifty years later. To name a few, C. J. Smith's *Intermediate Physics* was a leading text for over thirty years after its publication in 1931, while Peacock's *Elementary Microtechnique* published in 1934, stayed on the list until the late 1970s, as did *The Analysis of Engineering Structures* by Pippard and Baker, first published in 1937. Let us mention two more eminent authors whose works are still in print in one form or another. Ulick R. Evans wrote a number of books on metals of which *Metallic Corrosion, Passivity and Protection* was published in 1937; his later book *The Corrosion and Oxidation of Metals* (1960) is still in print. F. M. Lea first wrote *The Chemistry of Cement and Concrete* with C. H. Desch in 1934. The third edition, published in 1970, is still available, and this is truly remarkable in an age when the costs of warehousing and cataloguing hasten all but the most outstanding works to a premature recycling.

If the general publishing during the 1930s did not produce the same sort of gilt-edged list as the scientific, it was nonetheless still an active part of the firm's business, but this was the last decade in which this was so. Brian Fagan published no more fiction, apart from a few ghost stories. Some books, such as E. M. Forster's *Abinger Harvest* were a continuation of a long-established relationship, but a number of excellent new books were published, mainly in history, sport and current affairs.

The publication, in 1936, of *Abinger Harvest* produced a libel action, an improbable event in the history of the firm. The story was well told by Brian Fagan in a chapter he wrote, called "Forster and his Publishers" in *Aspects of E. M. Forster*, a collection of essays which we published, under the editorship of Oliver Stallybrass, to celebrate Forster's ninetieth birthday in 1969. We reprint this part of the essay in full, for the story is worth including in itself, and the extract illustrates Fagan's extremely clear, unpretentious, almost Forsterian style.

In 1936 Forster made a selection of his occasional papers – essays, reviews, broadcast talks – to be issued as a volume under the title *Abinger Harvest*. With it he sent me a few others to look through in case any might strike me as worth adding. One in particular seemed so brilliant and amusing that I asked him to put it in, and he consented to do so. In due course the collection was published and so the train was laid. The explosion occurred a few days after publication and took the form of letters to publisher and author from a firm of solicitors on behalf of Sir Murdoch MacDonald M.P., demanding withdrawal of the book and damages for libel in respect of the very article which I had persuaded Forster to include in it. This shock could not have come at a worse moment, for Forster was convalescent after an operation and in no condition to be worried by an affair of this kind. I drove down to Heytesbury, where he was staying with Siegfried Sassoon, and we agreed that I should get my firm's solicitors to defend the case on behalf of both of us and try to keep him out of it as far as possible. We had, of course, recalled all possible copies of the book and stopped the sale. When the solicitors got to work we had a further shock: they advised that the libel was unquestionable, there was no defence, and the only course was to settle on the best terms possible. This was duly done on the basis of an apology in court, agreed damages for charity, and costs, the article to be excised before the book was reissued.

What was this devastating article which we had so foolishly and so innocently reprinted? It was four pages long, was entitled "A Flood in the Office", and consisted of a review, contributed to *The Athenaeum* in 1919, of a pamphlet entitled *The Nile Projects*, written by Sir William Willcocks and published in Egypt in the same year. I have never seen the pamphlet itself, but it must have been inflammatory. To judge by what the reviewer wrote, it recorded an 'awful row' between two eminent engineers, expert on irrigation and water conservation, Sir William Willcocks and Sir Murdoch MacDonald, who had been advising the Egyptian Government about the treatment to be given to the River Nile. These opinions had evidently differed profoundly, and Sir William's wrath had boiled over into this pamphlet, in which he accused Sir Murdoch of having falsified statistics, suborned witnesses at an inquiry, and committed other unethical practices. The review, amusing and light-hearted, took the line that the rights and wrongs of the controversy must be left to the technicians to decide, but that the pamphlet had painted for the ordinary man a vivid picture of old Father Nile.

Our solicitors in 1936 discovered that soon after publication of the pamphlet in 1919 Sir William had been prosecuted for criminal libel in the Egyptian courts, convicted, and bound over to keep the peace – an event of which neither Forster nor I had, of course, ever heard. But unfortunately his review quoted some of Sir William's statements, and our reprint had therefore repeated the libel that had already been condemned some seventeen years before, and probably been forgotten by everyone else. It is easy to be wise now; and many may ask: "How could that hazard possibly have escaped you?" But perhaps one may be partly excused for having fallen into a trap that events had so cunningly set for us. Sir Murdoch behaved with propriety and without rancour, though he must have been furious, both personally and professionally, at the resurrection of the ghost he had thought to have laid for ever.

The tale has a happy ending: after the case was over, we were able to reissue *Abinger Harvest* without the offending passage, it started again on a long and successful life, and I was forgiven.

Abinger Harvest was the last book to be published by E. M. Forster until the appearance of *Two Cheers for Democracy* in 1951.

The sporting list covered many different topics from skiing to cricket. In this last (Herbert Sutcliffe's *For England and Yorkshire*, for example) Fagan was assisted by Reg Havercroft, who had joined the firm as General Manager in 1934. However, the most enduring part of the sporting list was undoubtedly the sailing books. The best were those by Adlard Coles, whose *Creeks and Harbours of the Solent* appeared in 1932, to be followed years later by *Channel Harbours and Anchorages*. (An earlier volume, *In Finnish Waters* was understandably less successful). The immaculate preparation of the charts appealed to Fagan, and the results have given pleasure and safe sailing to generations of yachtsmen.

The part of the general list closest to Fagan's own interests was history. One or two fairly popular books were included, such as J. D. Chamier's *Fabulous Monster*, a life of Kaiser William II, which sold extremely well in its German translation. Most of the list was more scholarly: Steven Runciman's *Byzantine Civilisation* was published in 1933, and this was thought of as being part of a series with W. W. Tarn's *Hellenistic Civilisation* (1927), and Harold Mattingly's *Roman Imperial Civilisation* which did not appear until 1957.

Probably the most important book to be published in the 1930s was H. A. L. Fisher's *A History of Europe*. The original publishers of this very famous work were Eyre & Spottiswoode, but Fisher (who had, at Lloyd George's request, left academic life towards the end of the Great War to become Minister of Education) insisted that it should also appear in a separate edition from a house with an educational list. Accordingly, a contract was exchanged in 1931 between Edward Arnold and E & S whereby we had the right, for the term of copyright, to publish a "cheaper" edition, in one volume, and to sell this throughout the British Empire. This was published in 1936, and was reprinted nine times in the following nine years. It was an important factor in improving the firm's position, and its standing in the trade.

This did, however, lead to trouble later on. Eyre & Spottiswoode's price was 54s net for a three-volume edition. The contract between them and us stipulated that the initial price for the Arnold edition should be around 12s 6d net, and our first actual price was 10s 6d net. This was gradually increased, in line with production costs, until, in 1949, a reprint was announced at 21s net. On 17

June 1949 Sir Charles Petrie wrote to Brian Fagan claiming that this constituted an infringement of copyright and a deliberate breach of the Agreement. He demanded the immediate withdrawal of all copies, and threatened to determine the licence altogether. E & S were by now publishing the work in two volumes, and at the substantially lower price of 40s net. From this, and from the aggressive tone of Sir Charles's letter, it was obvious to Fagan that the real motive of E & S was to get back the one volume edition for themselves, and he made this clear in the deposition he made to the High Court when the matter came to trial in April, 1950. Mr Justice Vaisey described the 1931 Agreement (drawn up by a firm of literary agents) as "exceedingly ill-drawn and lacking in certitude". He found that the problem related to the words "publish" and "cheaper": "publish" because it could and did refer both to the single act of putting the book on the market, and to the continuous act of keeping the book in print; and "cheaper" because it was not clear what the Arnold edition was to be cheaper than. He dismissed the action with costs, and a subsequent appeal was equally unsuccessful.

The affair might thus be said to have ended satisfactorily from an Arnold point of view, but it had caused a great loss of time and revenue to a small firm. The fact that copies had to be kept off the market for many months caused ill-will in the trade. Some idea of the importance of the matter can be gleaned from the fact that the temporarily undistributed reprint was for 28000 copies – a vast quantity in those days. Happily, the book recovered its position, and the one-volume Arnold edition sold in handsome numbers throughout the Empire until it was replaced by a paperback edition in the sixties.

Having successfully battled their way through the transfer of the partnership and the slump, Fagan and Dunn were no doubt hoping for better times. These, of course, were not to be, at any rate in the near future, and in 1939 they were faced with an entirely new set of problems.

The most immediate must have been the disappearance of staff into the armed forces. Many members were called up, including John Chandler, who had joined the firm in 1938, became warehouse foreman soon after his return at the end of the war, and completed 50 years with the company just before retiring. The most important absence was that of John Morgan; he had joined the Territorial Army in 1937, was called up on September 1st, 1939, and had an energetic and distinguished war career, ending it as a Lieutenant-Colonel. He returned to the office in November 1945.

A further disruption was the temporary removal of Fred Dunn and the Accounts Department, headed by the redoubtable Miss More, to Frome, in Somerset. This location was chosen because it was the headquarters of Butler and Tanner, who, at that time, were by far our most important printers. It was said that, from an Arnold point of view, sending a book to the printer and sending it to B & T were one and the same thing; and that one of B & T's machines had the notice "Edward Arnold only" permanently above it. Copy invoices were sent from London to Frome daily, and the firm's records were kept safely in the country, but the division of staff must have been cumbersome.

Brian Fagan and Reg Havercroft remained in London through-out the Blitz, mercifully without any direct damage to Maddox Street; one result of this was that we were able to help less fortunate publishers, including Longmans, by temporarily housing some of their stock. Our principal binders, James Burn, were twice bombed; their Kirby Street factory was destroyed in October 1940, as was their Farringdon Yard warehouse on 10 May, 1941 – the last great incendiary raid of the Blitz. They held a great deal of Arnold's unbound stock, and a very large number of the firm's titles were destroyed.

Another very serious problem, which was to last for ten years, was the shortage and consequent rationing of paper. The effect of this shortage (and of the destruction mentioned above) can be clearly shown in figures, for the Trade Catalogue for 1938 con-tained about 1800 titles, and that for 1945 about 1500, not all of which were currently available. This reduction was, of course, in spite of the addition of new books to the list. When considering these figures it must be remembered that in those days it was neither necessary nor customary to put books out of print merely because they sold slowly. It therefore follows that many of the titles which disappeared during the war (though some were reinstated afterwards) were books which should have been reprinted, but could not be. The shrinking of the list was thus a far more serious matter than a mere 16 per cent reduction of titles.

Joe Greener recalled that after the war he was asked to mark up the educational list, and found that an extraordinarily large number of titles were unavailable. No doubt the school books, so dependent on regular reprints, suffered worse than other sections of the list. The firm's publicity manager, Paul Edmonds, who had also been away at the war, remembered how exhausted the partners looked on his return, and how demoralizing it was to try to keep one's customers when one had nothing to sell.

In these circumstances Dunn continued to publish from Frome, but was not nearly as productive as he had been during the thirties. A few schoolbooks came out, one or two of great distinction such as C. P. Hill's *A History of the United States*, first published in 1940, third edition 1974, and still going strong in the late 80s. However, on looking through the catalogues, it is very striking to see how much of the publishing came from Tom Clare; indeed, it was a tremendous piece of good fortune for the firm that he was a little too old to be called up. He was active in school science (Nelkon: *Physics and Radio*, Penney: *Everyday Electricity and Magnetism* etc.); but even more so in the Technical Colleges, and technical books were what the wartime situation demanded. The books by W. A. J. Chapman (mostly still in print) are among the most successful ever published by Edward Arnold. *Workshop Technology* Part 1 was published in 1940, Parts 2 and 3 over the next few years. They had very large sales in the Arnold edition, and in the late 50s were among the first to be selected for the low-priced English Language Book Society scheme, in which edition they sold enormously in India and later in Africa. Tom also followed up the success of Gordon Sears's *Medicine for Nurses* with the even better selling *Anatomy and Physiology for Nurses*, and with *Materia Medica*, by the same author. All of these books, now under the editorship of R. S. Winwood, are still in print. During this time Tom Clare became the mainspring of Edward Arnold, and remained so until his death.

6

1945–1960

IN most ways the end of the war heralded a return to normality for the firm. The activities of the publishing trade as a whole were still restricted by paper rationing, but this became rather less stringent, and ended in 1949. Brian Fagan became President of the Publishers Association in 1945, which of course meant, in those days when the offices of Treasurer, President and Vice-President were held consecutively, that he was heavily involved in PA affairs for the six years 1943–49. One of his most important and demanding assignments was to be Chairman of the Paper Committee, which administered the rationing. The impartiality, and sometimes formidable integrity with which he handled this thorny problem earned him the respect of the Book Trade and, in 1949, a CBE. He knew how to be charming and severe at the same time; and he saw to it that Edward Arnold did not benefit from his position by so much as a quire.

With the return of F. P. Dunn and the accounts department from Frome the firm was once again all under the same roof. This was good news for most, but undoubtedly necessitated adjustments by some, as a certain camaraderie had naturally been encouraged by the circumstances of the war. In particular, after many nights of firewatching with the Senior Partner, Reg Havercroft began to entertain hopes of a partnership. The appointments, first of Tom Clare in 1944 and then of John Morgan on his return from the war (the announcement of which Havercroft was apparently left to read in *The Bookseller*) must have hit him hard, but he remained imperturbably kind and friendly to his subordinates.

The creation of two new partners was without doubt the most important act of the immediate post-war years. Fagan and Dunn

TRADE TERMS

The terms upon which goods will be supplied to the Home Trade are as follows:

BOOKS MARKED *

On Subscription or Journey { 25% from published price. / 5% settlement discount.

Otherwise, 2 or more copies of a title { 25% from published price. / No settlement discount.

„   single copies { At 2d. in 1/- from published price. / 5% settlement discount.

BOOKS MARKED §

On Subscription or Journey { At 2d. in 1/- from published price, less 2½%. / 5% settlement discount.

Otherwise   .   .   . { At 2d. in 1/- from published price. / 5% settlement discount.

ALL OTHER BOOKS

On Subscription or Journey { At 33⅓% from published price. / No settlement discount.

Otherwise, 2 or more copies of a title { At 33⅓% from published price. / No settlement discount.

„   single copies { At 25% from published price. / No settlement discount.

VOCAL MUSIC

On Subscription or Journey { At 25% from published price, less 5%. / 5% settlement discount.

Otherwise   .   .   . { At 25% from published price. / 5% settlement discount.

PIANOFORTE MUSIC

Novelty Rate or Journey { At half price. / No settlement discount.

Otherwise   .   . { At 33⅓% from published price. / No settlement discount.

3

How long did it take a bookshop to work out its discount in 1945?

had done a magnificent job of survival, but it is no criticism of them to say that they were not the men to seize the publishing opportunities which were opening up in the late nineteen forties. Their working life (struggle to continue the partnership, slump, war) had naturally made them cautious, and this caution was to serve them well in their new role of elder statesmen. They continued to publish, Dunn more than Fagan, but the development of the distinguished educational and professional lists, which gave the firm its identity for the next forty years, was the work of Tom Clare and John Morgan.

It has been related earlier that Tom Clare grew up with the firm; indeed he had been a powerful and successful figure since about 1930, with many publishing successes to his name. By the time he became a partner he was in his publishing prime and the next fifteen years saw him at his most productive. The extraordinary thing is not simply that he published in so many different fields (medicine at all levels – professional, student textbooks, books for nurses; engineering at university level; books for technical colleges, school science) but that he was able to score so many bull's-eyes in all of them.

In medicine he had, of course, inherited a number of very grand old books. To name a few: the Ten Teachers books *Obstetrics* and *Gynaecology* were first published as *Midwifery* and *Diseases of Women* in 1917 and 1919 respectively. Topley and Wilson's *The Principles of Bacteriology and Immunity* first appeared in 1929, Muir's *Textbook of Pathology* in 1924 and Mercer's *Orthopaedic Surgery* in 1932. All these titles were flourishing in revised editions during Tom Clare's time, and still are today. The revision of these vast tomes is in itself a daunting and time-consuming task but he took it in his stride and added many others.

Gordon Sears's *Medicine for Nurses* had been published in 1935, and the even more successful *Anatomy and Physiology for Nurses* in 1941. To these Tom now added Ellison Nash's *Surgery for Nurses*, which dominated its somewhat more specialised market for many years. Another outstanding text was Keith Simpson: *Forensic Medicine*, first published in 1947, ninth edition 1985. At professional level the years covered by this chapter saw the first publication of Greenfield's *Neuropathology,* 1958, as well as of a number of important works in the field of tropical medicine.

Tom Clare was equally productive in his other publishing fields. A few well-known and long-lived titles will give an impression of the scope: Rollason's *Metallurgy for Engineers*, Champion and Arnold: *Motor Vehicle Calculations*, a number of sixth form school science books by Nelkon and by Tyler, and at O level the extremely popular *Elementary Practical Physics*, 1954, by Draycott and Lyon. To appreciate Tom's creativity two things must be borne in mind: the books mentioned above represent only a fraction of his output; and his publishing activities were increasingly only a part of his broader responsibilities in the firm.

When John Morgan returned to Maddox Street in November 1945 to take up a partnership, he had been away at the war for just over six years. He had of course had seven years publishing experience before the war, most of it in school books, but in 1945 the situation had been vastly changed by R. A. Butler's 1944 Education Act. John was quick to grasp the opportunities that these changes would bring, and, particularly the new type of school book that would be required by the less academically gifted pupils in the new Secondary Modern schools.

To succeed in this new market John had to undertake something of a revolution in the firm. The traditional wisdom on school book publishing had been, at any rate since the Great War, that, firstly, good books were preferably written by masters at Winchester or Rugby, and secondly, that illustrations were expensive and unnecessary. If a picture had to be used in a book the print was subsequently put in the bottom drawer of a large chest in the main office, so that it could be used again. (In the 40s this was the domain of Mr Bertioli, a London Italian who detested Havercroft, but was an expert in the economical ordering of zincos: "Slap 'em up tight" was apparently all he needed to say to the blockmaker.) The present authors became very familiar with the contents of this drawer, which seemed to consist mainly of pictures of biplanes and the Throne room at Knossos.

It was clear that both these laws would have to be relaxed if the Secondary Moderns were to be conquered, and this took some doing; but eventually all was well, and the most striking and successful outcome was a series of four books called *Our World*, 1950 by E. W. Young and J. Mosby. This led to other books in similar format (Crown Quarto, illustrations on every page, either drawn or selected individually to reinforce the text, self-contained double-page spreads), notably Gunn's *Journey through History*. There were also many important Secondary Modern books of a more straightforward kind: for example, two series in English called *The Poet's Window* and *The Theatre Window* by a former fighter pilot called W. T. Cunningham.

John Morgan's publishing for Grammar and Technical schools was at least as distinguished as that for the Secondary moderns. In the field of history, Brandon, Hill and Sellman were all writers of real distinction, who wrote for our list both individually and together. Perhaps C. P. Hill's *Social and Economic History of Great Britain*, 1957, was (and is) the most outstanding. V. H. H. Green's first book *The Hanoverians* was a remarkable sixth form title. In Modern Languages *Histoires Illustrées* by Richardson and Fletcher (and several other titles by the same pair) had huge sales over a long period. In the technical schools A. E. Darbyshire's *The Craft of English* and Valerie Cliffe's *Making your own Clothes* made a successful and original contribution.

These prolific and forward-looking lists were accompanied by some more restrained and traditional publishing from the senior partners. F. P. Dunn continued the science list at an advanced level. Many of his reference books were substantial and distinguished, such as Charlesworth: *The Quaternary Era*, Evans: *The Corrosion and Oxidation of Metals*, and Graham: *The Sea Fisheries*. Dunn also kept a close eye on *Science Progress*, although during this time the increasing specialization of science was starting to make this journal, intended to make biology intelligible to physicists and so forth, less and less viable.

The general list, so important in the earlier days of the firm, was becoming somewhat marginal. It was, of course, a matter of deliberate policy to focus the firm's efforts on educational and academic publishing. However, the general list contained two active strands: the later works of E. M. Forster, and the residue of the sporting and games list. Forster's *Two Cheers for Democracy* was published in 1951, a collection of his previously published pieces. It received enormous critical acclaim and sold a very respectable number of copies in hardback, though it has to be confessed that a proportion of a rather too enthusiastic reprint spent a long life in the warehouse. *The Hill of Devi* followed in 1953. This was a charming minor work about Forster's early visits to India, interesting for itself, and as background to *A Passage to India*. The last work published by Forster before his death in 1970 was *Marianne Thornton*, a charming family memoir (1956). All these rather low-key books flourished in their Penguin editions.

The sporting and games list was not long to be continued, but it did include some classics in their fields such as *Reese on Play*, probably the most famous bridge book of its generation. Brian Fagan was also responsible for continuing the list of sheet music for schools, which had been started in 1918. The original editor, Thomas Dunhill, a well-known composer and a professor at the Royal College of Music, was married to Edward Arnold's daughter Mary. He was succeeded by Herbert Howells, who maintained a standard that was extremely high from an academic point of view, perhaps a little too much so for the market. After the war the overheads incurred in housing the list, and in employing someone (in the distinguished shape of an aristocratic Polish musician) to look out one sheet at a time at a probable list price of about fourpence proved unrealistic, and the list was sold to Novello in 1959.

The rapidly increasing publishing output was soon to have an effect on the organization of the business. The traditional role of the General Manager, whereby this powerful figure was responsible for all aspects of the firm except for the actual publishing and the finance became impossible, for with four partners wanting to see their books published as quickly as possible, it was all he could do to sustain the function of production manager. Reg Havercroft had found things difficult enough, but he left the firm in 1952 to become manager of the Epworth Press – an ideal appointment for a keen Methodist. He was succeeded as General Manager by Dennis Brunwin, whose experience was limited to accounts and production. The first change came on the sales side. This was accelerated by the publication of *Shakespeare, his World and his Work*, by Max Reese, a successful writer of school history books (and incidentally elder brother of Terence Reese of *Reese on Play*). This was a substantial book, aimed at the serious general reader. On the day of publication, in 1953, the author went to Blackwells, not unreasonably expecting to find a few copies of his work. No such luck – they had never heard of it. In view of its market the book was being published by Brian Fagan as part of the general list; but it was normal for Fagan to do a superlative editorial job, and then to lose all interest once it had been printed – "a good book sells itself". It therefore fell to John Morgan to stir things up. The outcome was the appointment of Anthony Hamilton as the first sales manager – a splendid stroke of luck for him but a curious choice since during his eighteen months with the company his experience had been largely in stock control and illustrations. He was accordingly summoned by the partners who told him that he was to have nothing to do with the appointment of representatives nor with the fixing of discounts but apart from that he was to get on with it and sell a hell of a lot of books. He remained nominally responsible to the General Manager, but in practice reported to the partners, so that the function of general manager became increasingly that of production and office manager.

Shortly after this, Bryan Bennett took charge of the sales of the educational list, reporting to John Morgan. He also had general office experience, but with particular responsibility for the distribution of inspection copies. The great importance of this was never fully understood by the partners other than John Morgan; they referred to the "give away" department, and were inclined to suggest to Bryan that his activities might with advantage be reduced. In fact they provided him with an ideal training for his future career. It is worth commenting that both these then young men were extremely fortunate to join the firm when they did. It is seldom possible nowadays for a young graduate to be given such a broad experience of the workings of a publishing house. Both the authors of this book feel a strong sense of gratitude to the partners of the early fifties for giving them such a sensible start.

Meanwhile, this period saw the first glimmerings of an appreciation of the importance to the firm of the export market. Neither of the senior partners was very interested in this nor, for that matter, in any kind of selling. Dunn never travelled at all but Fagan's Presidency of the PA led him to a certain involvement with overseas matters. He was Chairman of the Anglo-American Relations Committee which, in 1944, reached an agreement on the division of world markets with the American Bureau, later to become the American Book Publishers Council. A few years later Brian Fagan made a trip to North America with R. J. L. Kingsford, Secretary of the Cambridge University Press, and Fagan's successor as President of the PA. The visit did not seem to produce any commercial consequences for Edward Arnold, for Fagan would undoubtedly have felt it wrong for any such thing to have emerged from an official visit. Much later Fagan showed the present writer the menu they had been offered on the *Queen Mary*, with the sad comment that after years of rationing he and Kingsford had been unable to enjoy it.

Tom Clare made a trip to South Africa in 1948, which resulted in an Afrikaans edition of Sears's *Anatomy*, published by Juta, and a useful connection with Maskew Miller. It has to be said, however, that this trip and a much later one he made to the United States were nothing like as productive as his activities at home. By far the most significant of these early journeys was a long visit to Africa made in 1954 by John Morgan. In four months he went to Sierra Leone, the Gold Coast, Nigeria, South Africa (Pretoria only), Uganda, Tanganyika, Kenya, the Sudan and Egypt. Many good things came out of this, including P. E. H. Hair's *A History of West Africa*, the forerunner of our overseas list; and effective arrangements for representation in Nigeria, with Evans Brothers. However, in addition to the strain of a very long and exhausting trip, John Morgan incurred the displeasure of the Chairman. For Brian Fagan, all activities were divided into two kinds: "a job of work" such as proof-reading or manually calculating royalties, which was good; and "a day in the country" which was not. On his return from the the longest day in the country in the firm's history, John was simply told that a large number of jobs of work were awaiting his attention.

This was the extent of the major trips made between 1945 and 1960, but a number of overseas agencies were arranged during this time. Most of these were successful and lasted, sometime with changes, for many years, so that by 1960 the important regions of the world were fairly well covered. In North America the oldest, and by far the longest-living agency was for our medical books to be distributed in the United States by Williams and Wilkins of Baltimore. The arrangements between W & W and Edward Arnold have seen a few changes since they were first set up; but there has never been a time when business has not been done between the two companies, and it is a pleasure to write that the volume of trade is now greater than ever. In 1953, the agency in the United States for non-medical books was switched from Longmans to St Martin's Press, a new venture set up by Macmillan after their New York firm had broken loose from the parent. We also moved our Canadian business to Macmillan of Canada at the same time; this proved to be a very satisfactory relationship, which lasted over twenty years.

Two or three other arrangements are worth mentioning. In the late fifties the Straits Times of Singapore decided to set up a distribution company to cover South East Asia and Hong Kong. The first manager to be appointed was Sam Stewart, a friend of John Morgan, and Edward Arnold became one of the first agencies. It was a matter of some pride to both sides that an agency which was so effective for so long was based on an exchange of one-paragraph airletters. At about the same time we sent Major Chance to South Africa; this gallant figure, fresh from a military career, knew nothing about books or South Africa, but soon became a well-known and successful member of the trade. We also appointed Boxerbooks to sell our list in Europe, and this led, in 1958, to the company's first attendance at the Frankfurt Book Fair; our display on that occasion covered two shelves of a group exhibit.

Easily the most important of these export appointments came about soon after the war when a sergeant in the Royal Australian Air Force called at Maddox Street and succeeded in talking to the partners. His name was John Cochrane. He had had some experience in the Australian book trade before the war and he took home with him Agreements to represent three publishers exclusively in Australia and New Zealand: George Bell, E. & S. Livingstone and Edward Arnold. In those days our Australian sales were the smallest of the three, though this state of affairs was not to last. John Cochrane *was* Edward Arnold in Australia from 1946 until his retirement in 1973. Until 1964 he carried the three lists, with help only from his wife Olive, to the bookstores, and directly to schools, colleges and universities throughout the continent. Every January he filled his station wagon with sample copies and spent three months doing the same thing in New Zealand, covering both islands from top to bottom. The fifties were the heyday of

British book sales to Australia, since the local publishing trade (especially educational) was only just beginning to develop. John Cochrane made the most of this not only by securing very large adoptions for Edward Arnold school books but also in producing authors for us in Australia and New Zealand. This was a two way traffic. The anthologies compiled by Bill Smyth, for example, especially *Poems of Spirit and Action*, sold splendidly in Britain and the rest of the Commonwealth, as well as in the author's native New Zealand.

John Cochrane's importance to Edward Arnold cannot be exaggerated, for as well as producing excellent sales he played a large part in waking the firm up to the possibilities of export. He once related how shocked he had been when the then general manager had told him he need only send his orders in "every week or so". His reply is not recorded, but on the receiving end, it was obvious that he airmailed a bundle almost every evening.

The fifties was an active but fairly tranquil time in publishing as a whole; the flurry of mergers and acquisitions which characterized the sixties and all subsequent decades had hardly begun. At the end of this period the firm was still financed entirely by the funds which the partners (later directors) had invested in the business and an annually renewable overdraft from Coutts – there was no permanent external capital. In 1953 the partnership was transformed into a private limited company. The four partners sold the goodwill and available assets of the partnership to a new company, which had to be called Edward Arnold (Publishers) Ltd, as an Edward Arnold Ltd already existed. They then took out service agreements with the new company. It is interesting to note that each of the four directors was in charge of a publishing department, any other form of activity being considered unworthy of a member of the Board. The company was capitalised at £115 000, of which £55000 was represented by ordinary shares and £60000 by preference shares. The goodwill of the partnership was valued at £35000.

This had no immediate effect on the funding or control of the company, which continued to be run as a virtual partnership for years to come. The notion of external funding aroused no enthusiasm, but by the late 1950s it could no longer be ignored. This was partly due to the expansion of the business, but mainly because Brian Fagan announced that he planned to retire at the end of 1960, and Fred Dunn at the end of 1962. Both, naturally enough given their own past experience, wished to take out the bulk of their holdings (at least that part represented by ordinary shares) in cash, and there was no possibility of the younger directors being able to raise this.

Accordingly, various discussions were held with merchant banks. On the whole these served to confuse the directors whose collective experience in such matters was nil and who at that time lacked effective financial advice. One bank, a leader in its day, produced a complicated scheme whereby we were to sell 51 per cent of 51 per cent of the equity, thus losing control. Mercifully it was realized in time that the bank had little or no interest in the future of Edward Arnold but a good deal of interest in making an experiment. It was decided not to proceed with this scheme and not long afterwards the company came to rest in the safe hands of the Industrial and Commercial Finance Corporation (ICFC), as it was then known, and more particularly of its sub-division the Estate Duties Investment Trust, known as Edith. This proved for many years to be a happy relationship partly because it was the policy of ICFC not to take a majority interest, and not to interfere in the running of the company as long as the results were satisfactory. Their first investment produced funds for the retirement of the two senior partners, and a further modest sum for the expansion of the business. It was to be the first investment of several over a period of about twenty five years.

Once it became apparent that Fagan and Dunn were actively planning to retire, the four directors began to consider the future of the Board. It had become a tradition – and a very sensible one – that the partners/directors were appointed in pairs, with one arts man (Fagan, Morgan) and one scientist (Dunn, Clare). The intention was to continue this scheme, and two young men were invited to join the Board with effect from January 1958. With typical thoughtfulness, they were given about two years notice of this to enable them to work out the necessary financial arrangements and also to have easier contact with the existing directors. During this period however, it became apparent that the behaviour of the scientist was so erratic that a Board appointment would really not be suitable. Anthony Hamilton therefore joined the

Board at the agreed time on his own, but remained so only until he was joined by Bryan Bennett in 1962.

Anthony had been invited to start a new list for the Arts side of university studies. This contained the remnants of the general list and was much fortified by John Morgan who generously handed over to the new list several of his successful higher level texts of which V. H. H. Green's *Renaissance and Reformation* is a splendid example. This gave the list credibility as well as turnover, but Anthony found on his university visits that the company's reputation as a publisher in other fields was so high that he had little difficulty in persuading people to write.

There was now a gap on the science side. The departed editor had been an engineer and had commissioned some good books during his time with the company. He was replaced by L. C. "Sam" Selwood, an Engineer Lieutenant Commander in the Royal Navy. However, the retirement of Fred Dunn would leave the company without a pure science publisher and it was decided also to remedy this. Here chance intervened. Fred Dunn had long since formed a friendship with E. G. Carpenter of Coutts, by this time general manager at 440 Strand. Dunn had put Carpenter up for membership of the Savile Club and over one of their regular lunches it emerged that Carpenter had a stepson who had gone into teaching after reading biology at Cambridge but was getting restless. Paul Price was therefore interviewed by the Directors, was offered the position of science editor, and joined the firm in this capacity in 1960. The choice of a biologist was fortunate, for biology was then beginning its position of dominance among the sciences, a position it was to hold for about twenty years.

Brian Fagan retired, as planned, at the end of 1960. It marked the end of an era, though not abruptly as Fred Dunn continued for two more years as Chairman. Fagan had joined the firm in 1919; he became a partner in 1921, senior partner in 1930, and Chairman in 1953. He was not a prolific publisher (though much of his output was distinguished) nor was he really a businessman by temperament. He had a first class analytical mind with a formidable ability to put his finger on the weak spot in any argument; but this was always applied gently, and with a quizzical sense of fun: "Look at this estimate, Hamilton; Sam wants to print a lot of copies . . . so that he can sell them". He steered the company through an extremely difficult time, and left it in excellent shape. He had been appallingly injured on the Somme in 1916, and, not surprisingly, he began to show his age a little towards the end of the fifties. It is therefore pleasant to record that he had over a decade of happy retirement, dying in 1971 at the age of 77.

7

1961–1977

1961–1965

AFTER Brian Fagan's retirement Fred Dunn, then in his
seventies, took on the Chairmanship for two years.
Although several years older than Fagan he had always
been second partner or director, and he was very anxious to be
head of the firm, if only for a short time. From the point of view
of the youngest members of the Board this was a success, for
F.P.D. was approachable and receptive, and in any case left the
day-to-day running of the business to his colleagues. It was perhaps
not such an easy time for Tom Clare and John Morgan, Tom
being already in his late fifties, and John a few years younger. Tom
became Chairman on Dunn's retirement at the end of 1962, and
remained so until his untimely death in 1965.

Bryan Bennett, by this time in control of educational publishing
as well as selling, joined the Board in 1962. Paul Price became a
director two years later, in charge of the company's scientific, but
not, at that stage, of its medical programme.

Fred Dunn's contribution to the company was in many ways as
great as Brian Fagan's, and was complementary to it. They did
not seem to become close personal friends, but formed a very
effective team. He was more outgoing than Fagan, and enjoyed
taking authors to the Savile for lunch (whereas Fagan was often to
be seen showing them out of the front door at 1.45 p.m., and then
going round the corner for a sandwich on his own); but he was

also more irascible, and did not hesitate to shout at employees in the main office if a book went out of stock, or an electro was fuzzy. In private he was very kind and generous, and for several years after his retirement he attended the AGM, and was supportive to his successors. He was also an exceptional scientific publisher, and one of the first to be a scientist of some distinction in his own right. He possessed a legendary ability to print precisely the right number of copies of a seemingly obscure title.

The first half of the 60s was a very positive period for the company. Turnover and profits went up very steadily, both showing a growth of over 70 per cent between 1960 and 1965. The net profit before tax ran at an average of 18 per cent of turnover, with a peak of 22 per cent. This was, of course, the result of sound publishing in the past, assisted by an increasingly active new book programme.

The school book department reaped the harvest of John Morgan's activity since the war, and also began to benefit from Bryan Bennett's new contacts. After the success of *Our World*, mentioned above, Bill Young turned (with a new partner in the shape of John Lowry) to a multi-volume GCE series, *A Course in World Geography*. The first volume was published in 1960, and the series held the predominant place in grammar school geography teaching for over twenty years. Another extremely successful venture was *Practical Cookery* by Victor Ceserani and Ronald Kinton. This was first published in 1962, and was followed in 1964 by *The Theory of Catering*. Both books, now in their seventh and sixth editions respectively, became and have remained the standard texts in their field; together they have sold nearly one and a quarter million copies. These two books, with others by the same authors, formed the cornerstone of Arnold's catering list.

The science list was also very active. Paul Price was quick to get off the mark in biology. One of his first successes was *The Mechanism of Heredity* (1965), by H. L. K. Whitehouse, reviewed as the best genetics text for a generation. This immediately raised the company's profile as significant publishers in biology as did our importation of *Molecules to Man*, the most rigorous of three texts issued by the Biological Sciences Curriculum Study (BSCS) in the United States. On the technical side Sam Selwood was engaged in producing a series to cover the new TEC courses, which required the subject to be broken down into smaller topics than had formerly been the case.

Medical sales continued to flourish, though the flow of new books was not as great as it had been in the 50s, for the good reason that Tom Clare's time was now taken up with running the business. His first attempt to appoint a successor was not entirely successful, but this underlined the point that medical publishing, by means of revised editions, has a stronger built-in life than any other form of publishing except legal.

The humanities department began to take shape with some significant books in English literature (*Stratford-upon-Avon Studies*, edited first by John Russell Brown and Bernard Harris), English language (Gimson: *Introduction to the Pronunciation of English*), history (Elliott: *Imperial Spain*, Steinberg's *Dictionary of British History*, Pollard: *Development of the British Economy*), and, perhaps most interestingly, geography. This had for long been a very dull subject, most of the available textbooks being descriptive and regional. Arnold's image as a geography publisher was transformed by a visit from Peter Haggett, which led to the publication of his *Locational Analysis in Human Geography*, the first synthesis of the then new quantitative approach to the subject. *New Society* welcomed it as "the most original and important book from a British geographer for many years".

The early sixties also saw an increase in travel by the directors. In 1963 Bryan Bennett made a mammoth seven week journey around Africa, the first visit to that continent since the one made by John Morgan nine years earlier. Among many other activities he established a fruitful co-publishing arrangement with Juta in South Africa, and recruited several South African authors. Later in the same year Tom Clare visited the United States, concentrating on our medical business with Williams & Wilkins. In the following year John Morgan made a long and important tour of Australia and New Zealand. John Cochrane was still covering both countries, but it was apparent that this was now too much for one man, not on account of any failing in John Cochrane's powers, but because the business had been so greatly expanded by him. John Morgan therefore made two important changes. The first was to hive off New Zealand as a separate territory, and to appoint Derek Atkinson to be our representative (a successful appointment which lasted for nearly twenty years); the second was to hold stock in Australia for the first time. This was, to begin with, a "life-line" arrangement, and did not involve closing the market; but it did involve forming a limited company for purposes of trading, and this, in turn, led to the not entirely happy transformation of John Cochrane from salesman into administrator. The amount of business done through our stocks held in Melbourne quickly became a large proportion of total sales. Also in 1964, Anthony Hamilton made the first of many visits to North America, visiting campuses as well as agents. At that time we were very well represented in Canada by Macmillan, but in the States St Martin's Press had been going through a difficult time. The new President of the company was Frank Upjohn, from Toronto; he was concerned to improve the performance of their college department, but agreed to loosen the Arnold arrangement with St Martin's, so that we could place books elsewhere if it seemed desirable to do so.

Apart from the changes to the Board outlined earlier there was an important alteration to the senior staff structure. Dennis Brunwin left the company early in 1964 to take up an appointment with a printer. His departure caused the end of the position of general manager, which had at one time been so vital, but had become something of an anachronism. Brunwin was replaced as production manager by Jim Girling, while the office management side of the job went to Mike Husk, who had started his employment in the trade department, and had later moved into production. This experience was to prove valuable when we established a separate distribution centre four years later.

The expansion of the company outlined above naturally created considerable pressure on space. At the beginning of the 1960s the entire staff was housed under one roof at 41/43 Maddox Street, with forward stocks held in the basement, and reserve stocks in the crypt of St George's, Hanover Square. This arrangement was economical but archaic. The annual stocktaking had to be carried out by candlelight, while the fact that it was difficult to move more than one parcel of books out of reserve at one time was good for stock control, but less so for service. It could also occur, that if the Arnold storeman pulled the wrong switch in the crypt, the organ supporting a grand society wedding would groan to an embarrassing halt. It was desirable to stay put in Maddox Street, not only for the location, but because the property was held on a twenty one year lease (1951–1972) at a very reasonable rent. The first answer to the space problem was therefore to make more room for stocks by clearing the ground floor main office in Maddox Street and redistributing some of the departments as necessary. To this end office accommodation was taken in Hanover Square, and first the accounts department and later the education and publicity departments were moved there. This temporary arrangement proved less than satisfactory, especially for those who had been moved out of Maddox Street.

The first funds from ICFC, more for retirements than for working capital, arrived in March 1961. The high level of activity during the following years brought a need for more funds, and at the end of 1965 ICFC took up a further 80 000 preference shares and a further 5000 ordinary shares, increasing their equity holding to 37.5 per cent.

In October 1965 Tom Clare died suddenly of a heart attack. This was a shattering blow to the company, both in business and personal terms. Some indication has already been given of his exceptional talents as a publisher; perhaps the best evidence of this is that the medical list is still benefiting from his books, twenty five years after his death. He was also an outstandingly vigorous and capable head of the company, and it is tragic that he only held this position for three years. To those who were lucky enough to work closely with him the experience was a delight. He was always approachable, came swiftly to the point, and made rapid, sensible and generous decisions; and, as if that wasn't enough, he was fun to be with.

1966–1971

Tom Clare's death left John Morgan as the only surviving member of his generation, a situation which cannot have been easy for him. In announcing the loss of Tom, he appointed himself to be Chairman, and Anthony Hamilton to be Managing Director. It was the first time that such a vulgar term had been used in the firm.

There was a great deal for the Board to do, and by far the most pressing item was to find appropriate accommodation for our

warehouse and distribution departments. The arrangements described above were becoming increasingly unworkable, and the
matter was now very urgent. Other publishers had been through
the same problem, and some had apparently benefited from the
advice of management consultants; we therefore decided to use the
services of such a firm, one which we knew to have had a great
deal of relevant experience.

Given the pressure on the directors after Tom's death, this was
a very sensible plan, but it did not work out quite as we had hoped.
The first surprise was that the consultant appointed to us – a very
pleasant young man – had no experience of warehouse moving,
and the second surprise was that this was presented as a deliberate
decision. He duly beavered away for three months and came up
with an elegantly presented report, which told us that we were
educational publishers who wished to move our warehouse out of
London, but preferably not to Pembrokeshire or Caithness. It
would be tedious to recite all the reports which were produced.
To cut a long story short, we came very close to acquiring leasehold
accommodation in Wokingham in 1967. We had hoped for a
freehold, but were assured that nothing suitable was available at a
reasonable price. We were saved from the leasehold fate by the
developer, who insisted on including in the contract an entirely
unacceptable clause, which would have made it compulsory for us
to lease an additional space after three years, whether or not we
required it.

There was an element of good luck in this, but it also meant
that we would have to survive another season in our antiquated
London premises. It was greatly to the credit of our distribution
management and staff that we did so. The consultant was told to
scour the country west of London, but not further than Reading,
for freehold properties, and on a tour of inspection the following
week the first building we viewed was Woodlands Park. It was
not a grand establishment: it had been a baked beans factory, and
a gaping hole had been left in a section of the roof, to allow the
fumes to escape. However, the location suited us admirably, and
there was room for expansion; with some reconstruction and
extension it became the home of all the distributive aspects of the
business for twenty years.

After completion of the purchase the consultants asked for a meeting; they suggested that, as we must obviously be delighted with their performance, we should continue with them for the period of moving in, at an increased fee. We found it easy to decide that we should prefer to make our own mistakes in future, and terminated the assignment.

We appointed Mike Husk to be the resident director in charge of Woodlands, his previous experience having made him a natural choice for the job. He and several managers moved to Berkshire, and we had little difficulty in engaging suitable, if inexperienced staff. We opened shop at Woodlands at Easter, 1968.

The move to Woodlands coincided with a rather difficult time in the history of the company. The move itself naturally involved us in considerable expenditure, while a temporary slowing up in the momentum of our sales (common to the book trade at that time) led to a drop in profitability. This was also a time of takeovers in publishing; many small and medium-sized firms found themselves the object of usually undesirable attentions, and Edward Arnold was no exception. These advances had started in the early sixties, but increased in number and earnestness towards the end of the decade. We were desperately keen to remain independent, and confident that we could make a go of it, but the combination of circumstances mentioned above meant that our position was precarious, at least for the time being. What should we do?

The first step was to secure our situation at the bank. ICFC were being supportive, but considered that our problem should best be solved by an extended overdraft. To the surprise of everyone, including our bank manager, the Board of Coutts initially turned down our request. At this point the directors felt that for the first time we should invite an outsider to join us on the Board in a part time capacity, someone who had far more experience of the City than any of us. On considering candidates, John Morgan came up with the suggestion of Eric Carpenter, in some ways an ideal choice. He was admirably suited to cope with the Bank, having himself been General Manager of Coutts; and he was likely to take a sympathetic interest in our problems as he was Paul Price's stepfather. We therefore had talks with Eric, who agreed to join our Board for a year or two. His first act was a successful appeal to the Bank to increase our facility.

This held the situation for the time being, but there remained the more serious problem of long term funding. The difficulty was that if ICFC were to increase their holding substantially, there would be a risk of this approaching 50 per cent; and, apart from being undesirable from our point of view, this was not part of their policy. We therefore had to consider very carefully the takeover proposals being put to us, as the sums involved were far beyond the resources of the directors, and John Morgan, looking ahead to retirement, was hoping to reduce his holding in the firm.

At about this time John introduced to us an old friend of his called Bill Tomkinson, an eminent accountant. An able and impressive man, he at first appeared to the younger directors as rather an ogre. This impression was quickly dispelled once "Tomsk" had satisfied himself about the company's operations. He became an extremely constructive friend to us, and a most valuable advisor. Some years later the audit was moved to his own firm, Ball, Baker, Deed.

The rest of 1968 and the first months of 1969 were much taken up with discussions about the future. By far the most attractive of the various takeover approaches came from Heinemann Educational Books, at that time, along with the rest of the Heinemann group, under the benevolent ownership of Thomas Tilling. HEB was a distinguished and very successful educational publishing house, the creation of Alan Hill. In such a merger we would have been in sympathetic company, but the younger members of the Board in particular were determined on independence, and doubtful (rightly, as it turned out later) of the wisdom of surrendering control to a company which might itself be sold. Alternatives, however, were not readily apparent.

The crucial meeting took place in a private room at Brown's Hotel, and was attended by the Arnold Board, including Eric Carpenter, plus Bill Tomkinson. The atmosphere was tense, to say the least, but relieved by excellent food and drink. (At that time John Morgan had a rather grand secretary, who, when ordering lunch on the telephone, said "Oh, and we'd better have a few bottles of decent claret". This turned out to be Haut Brion.)

John Morgan was not keen on a sale as such, but could see no alternative. Eric Carpenter felt sure we could not succeed on our own. Eventually Anthony said he had a friend who might be interested in taking up shares in Edward Arnold, and in introducing other shareholders to ensure a private majority. This was immediately welcomed by Tomsk as being a positive idea, and the meeting closed with Anthony being given two weeks to come up with a proposal.

The friend in question was James Martyn. We had been aware for some time of James's interest in publishing, and in small companies. He had been a founder of Newman Neame, and later became Chairman for some years. However, as by 1969 he had sold the company, and no longer had any conflicting ties in publishing, it seemed an appropriate time to approach him. After a number of meetings a plan was put forward to the Arnold Board, and James was introduced to the directors, and to the company's advisors and bankers. With the support of ICFC the problem was quickly solved. ICFC increased their holding of Convertible Preferred Ordinary shares to 42.5 per cent; more importantly, there was also a new issue of Ordinary shares, with the arrangement that any shares not taken up would be offered to James and his squad of shareholders at a small premium.

This was the first step in an arrangement which was to last very happily for eighteen years. James joined the Company in October 1969, and the Board in February of the following year, on the retirement of Eric Carpenter. His selection of shareholders was brilliant; none had a large holding, but together they enabled the Company to maintain an independent majority; in addition to this, several of them were able, by virtue of their own activities and interests, to be extremely helpful to the Company. They were a constant source of support to the management.

It is true that corporate affairs of one sort or another tended to be uppermost in the directors' minds during this period. However, there was plenty of activity of a more normal, publishing kind. Although sales flattened out in the late sixties, they then increased again sharply, so that the turnover in 1971 was 64 per cent greater than in 1965. The profits took a dive in 1968, as has already been mentioned; but they started to recover again satisfactorily in 1970.

In most respects the publishing programme was very active and successful. Paul Price continued to develop the science list, with emphasis on biology. This was a time of series publishing, and two notable examples were launched in the late sixties. *Studies in Biology*, sponsored by the Institute of Biology, came out with three titles in 1966, the first of which, *Ecological Energetics* by John Phillipson was exceptionally successful, and achieved very large sales as an Open University prescribed text. The series published its one hundredth title in 1978: *Cellular Recognition in Plants* by J. Heslop-Harrison, and in that year sales of the series reached one million copies. In 1967 the *Contemporary Biology* series was also started with a winner, Aubrey Manning's *Animal Behaviour* which was particularly successful in the United States.

The medical list continued to produce profitable turnover, but was undernourished with new books as both our first two attempts to support or replace Tom Clare were failures. At this point it was decided to offer the job to Paul Price, who, as a biologist, was some way towards understanding the subject, and, as a director of the company, carried sufficient weight to work with medical authors. He accepted, and took on the medical list in 1970, continuing to oversee the science publishing. For the first eighteen months he had the enthusiastic support and advice of Gordon Signy, a distinguished pathologist who had recently retired; but this splendid arrangement was sadly cut short by Gordon's sudden death in 1971.

The educational list continued to be our largest and most profitable area under Bryan Bennett. The hallmark of his publishing was that we should have the essential course texts in as many subject areas as possible. Mathematics provides a good example of this. We had a course for secondary modern schools, *Discovering Mathematics* by Alan Shaw and F. E. Wright; a traditional grammar school course, *Certificate Mathematics* by R. W. Fox; and, introduced by John Morgan, a series for the "New Maths" called *Contemporary School Mathematics*. This was under the editorship of G. Matthews of St Dunstan's College, and was in direct competition with the powerful Nuffield series. All three of these multi-volume courses sold in large numbers.

Another important plank in the secondary list was the establishment of a wide-ranging series of up to date anthologies, known as *The World of English*; this meant that at any one time we would have five or six major prescriptions for school examinations, in the UK and in other Commonwealth countries. In addition to this, Bryan also developed our list in the rapidly growing field of Further Education, and made a start in publishing for the teaching of English as a foreign language with the first of several books by Ona Low: *A First Certificate English Course* (1967).

In the humanities department the academic programme was further developed, particularly in history (*Foundations of Modern History*, edited by A. Goodwin) and geography (Harvey: *Explanation in Geography*). Also through Peter Haggett came a series called *Progress in Geography*. This was initially published as a series of books only because at that time we did not feel ready to set up a Journals department; but a few years later the series was converted into our first journals since the sale of *Science Progress*, by John Davey, who had joined the department in 1967.

There was also activity of a more general kind. E. M. Forster died in 1970. The literary executorship went to King's College, Cambridge, where Forster had spent much of his later life as a Fellow. At a meeting with the Executors it was agreed, at our suggestion, that the bulk of Forster's work, published and unpublished, should appear in a scholarly edition under the editorship of Oliver Stallybrass. There were good commercial, as well as literary, reasons for this proposal, for the novels and other published works existed only in a pocket edition; this was rather attractive, but the texts, printed just after the war, were far from impeccable, and from a sales point of view the pocket books had long since been eclipsed by the Penguin edition. Penguin agreed to convert their own edition to the *Abinger Edition* (as our new series was called) as and when our volumes appeared, and stocks of their current paperbacks were exhausted.

At the meeting it was also revealed that certain of Forster's works had not been published during his lifetime as they dealt with homosexual themes, and had been written at a time when publication would have been unacceptable, even if not illegal. The most important of these was *Maurice*, a novel completed after some delays in 1914, but revised in 1919, 1932 and 1959–60. It would have been possible to have published it after the last revision, but Forster did not wish to do so, as by then he felt it to be remote. It was agreed that this should now be published as quickly as possible, as a separate item from the *Abinger Edition*, which it might join later. The book was published in 1971, receiving great interest

92

and mixed opinions. It was exciting, at Edward Arnold, to be publishing an important work of fiction, so long after the firm had ceased doing this, and forty seven years after publication of *A Passage to India*. Forster's American and foreign language rights had always been handled separately, by himself. The US publisher of *Maurice* was W. W. Norton, with whom we were on the friendliest of terms. In Canada, the Macmillan Company decided to produce their own edition of 3500 copies, under licence from Arnold. We printed 21500 copies, of which about 17000 sold extremely quickly, and a proportion of the remainder extremely slowly. Apart from the appearance in the following year of a collection of Forster's short stories, *The Life to Come*, this was our only excursion into fiction publishing.

The move to Woodlands was a great success, but we discovered that a few procedural changes were necessary. One of the most important of these concerned the method of invoicing. In London we had relied on a small number of splendid clerks, who knew the list backwards, and had no difficulty in preparing a manual invoice very quickly, largely out of their heads. Obviously the newly recruited staff at Woodlands could not be expected to have the same knowledge, so after two or three weeks of listening to cries of "Who wrote *A Passage to India*?" we decided that the age of the machine had arrived. We acquired three automatic invoicing machines which operated from punched cards; the tape they produced, which was processed by a bureau, provided us with an adequate sales analysis by title and market.

It was decided, with strong encouragement from Bill Tomkinson, that we should employ a fully fledged chartered accountant. Tomsk himself produced a short list for us, and we had no difficulty in selecting Jim Peck, who had been working for Heinemann Educational Books – an ideal background for his job with Edward Arnold. In the sixteen years he spent with us he made a very valuable contribution to the company, first as Accounts Manager, then, in 1973, joining the Board as Financial Director.

Other Board changes took place around 1970. Bryan Bennett took over the sales and marketing responsibilities, bringing new ideas to the job; he consequently withdrew from his direct management of school books, though he continued with certain projects such as the Schools Council's seminal *Language in Use*. Nicolas

McDowall, who had been with the company for several years, first as a representative and then as an editor, joined the Board in 1971, in charge of the school book department.

Also in 1971, at his own request, John Morgan retired as Chairman, handing over this position to Anthony Hamilton. John had suffered from ill health during the late sixties, and was anxious to lead a quieter life without losing touch with the company. He therefore remained on the Board for a further five years as President. He regularly attended not only Board meetings, but also meetings of the Editorial Committee, and at these in particular he plainly enjoyed himself, playing an extremely helpful and constructive role.

John was the founder of Arnold's post-war school book publishing; under his direction it became, and long remained the most substantial and profitable publishing department in the firm. By his work for the Publishers Association he was instrumental in raising the profile of educational publishers, both inside and outside the trade. From 1917 when the Educational Group of publishers first met in Maddox Street, Edward Arnold was one of the leading twelve educational publishers, and one of the top six secondary publishers. In 1933 this group was formalized as Group III of the Publishers Association, and John Morgan played an active part in this from 1946 onwards. In the mid-sixties a number of younger publishers (from Arnold, Ginn, HEB, Murray, Nisbet and Schofield and Sims) met on a regular, informal basis, to discuss the current needs of educational publishers which they felt were not being met by Group III. John Morgan, Alan Hill and John Mackenzie Wood were understanding and supportive. As a result, the Morgan-Wood committee was set up in 1967 to examine the workings of Group III. Its recommendations were accepted, and in 1969 the Educational Publishers Council was inaugurated as a full division of the PA.

1972–1977

One result of moving our distribution and accounts to Woodlands Park in 1968 had of course been that we were enabled to bring all the rest of the company under one roof again, in Maddox Street.

This was a great improvement, but three years later we found it necessary to make another move, in London. There were several reasons for this. Business was expanding again; the Maddox Street buildings, designed by Arnold as a complete publishing house, with space for stocks and a flat for the caretaker, were less suitable now that they were used for nothing but offices; and the lease was due to expire in 1972. We therefore searched for suitable London properties during 1971 – not a very easy task in the middle of the Heath government's short-lived housing boom. We eventually found, and acquired the lease of, 25 Hill Street, a handsome Mayfair house built in 1830. It was our hope and expectation that this would be our head office for many years to come.

The recovery in our sales and profits, which had started in 1970, continued in 1972, and indeed, except for a dip in 1974/5, progressed steadily until the end of the decade. It became more difficult to make sense of the figures as we were entering the period of great inflation; but since our sales revenue multiplied by 3.8 between 1970 and 1978, and our profit figure by 4.3, it is safe to assume that there was a considerable element of real increase. In 1975 we increased our working capital for the first time since 1969. This took the form of a loan and an increase in equity, including a rights issue which still left the directors and private shareholders with a majority. In the three following years both sales and profits went up sharply, profits breaking the half million mark for the first time.

One of the most interesting developments of this period occurred in Australia. Bryan Bennett made an important visit in 1972, during which it was agreed that John Cochrane should retire at the end of 1973, and that Bill Hunter, formerly a director of James Nisbet, should go out early that year to work himself in with a view to taking over as Managing Director in 1974. This duly took place: we acquired the share capital of John Cochrane Pty Ltd, and renamed the company Edward Arnold Australia. Apart from the logic of the acquisition there was a business reason behind this decision. John Cochrane was extremely well-known as a salesman but the plan was that we should now start to publish in Australia and for this purpose the name of the parent company was obviously more suitable.

John Cochrane had been with us for nearly thirty years, and

during that time had built up Arnold's presence in Australia from nothing to the point where we were able to establish our own company; in all of this he was capably supported by his wife, Olive. In retirement they continued to live in their house in Albert Park, John looking after the houses he owned in the neighbourhood and making fairly frequent visits to the race-track. He died in 1984.

At home we were spending a good deal of time in discussing whether or not to install a computer at Woodlands Park. The invoicing machines had served us well, and had enabled us to make a start on a regular sales analysis; however, they were relatively slow and their function was limited. There were three possibilities: to add a fourth invoicing machine; to put ourselves entirely in the hands of a service bureau; or to acquire our own computer. To our delight the sums pointed unequivocally to the purchase of a computer. This, a Singer, later absorbed in the UK by ICL, arrived in the autumn of 1973 and went live on 1 May, 1974. This was an extremely smooth operation, for which the credit belongs to Jim Peck, who masterminded it, and to Brian Jones, our Data Processing Manager. He had joined us two or three years earlier and thus was familiar with our business, as well as being on top of the technical side. The invoicing and most accounting functions were absorbed with no hitches (though royalties were not computerised until several years later); while the sales analysis was made far more valuable by showing the cost of sales, by title and by sales area.

During these years Paul Price began to revitalize the medical list after its brief spell in the doldrums. In 1974 the first two volumes in the series *Current Topics in Immunology* appeared, under the editorship of Professor John Turk. Another important step was the publication, in 1976, of the first volume of *Current Surgical Practice*, edited on behalf of the Royal College of Surgeons by John Hadfield and Michael Hobsley. This volume and its successors were "essential reading for all Fellowship candidates" (*British Journal of Surgery*) and sold very well in the United Kingdom, and all countries where the FRCS examination is taken.

This medical publishing activity naturally made it impossible for Paul to remain equally productive in science, and we were joined by John Roberts, who at first took over the non-biological sciences, reporting to Paul, but later became head of all scientific publishing, including, after the retirement of Sam Selwood, the engineering side. There was no lack of biological publishing, however; the two big series, started in the sixties, continued to provide important new titles and new editions: *The Biology of the Protozoa* by John Sleigh and *The Principles and Techniques of Practical Biochemistry* edited by B. L. Williams and K. Wilson are good examples.

In the humanities department John Davey, who left us in 1977 to join Basil Blackwell, was extremely productive. Much was published in geography, a subject in which we were market leaders during the seventies: an excellent example is *The Ecology of Natural Resources* by Ian Simmons. The most important event for the history list was the appearance, starting in 1977, of *The New History of England* under the very distinguished editorship of A. G. Dickens and Norman Gash. The first volume to be published was G. R. Elton's *Reform and Reformation*.

It had long been our intention to add a list of journals to our academic publishing programme. Journals and books complement and feed each other in many ways, while journals have the advantage that, if successful, they become self-funding. The existence of the *Progress in Geography* series, mentioned earlier, made it natural that, once the green light had been given, Humanities should be first at the starting line. Two journals, *Progress in Human Geography* and *Progress in Physical Geography* were launched in 1977, joined by the related, but entirely new and separate *International Journal of Urban and Regional Research*. The mechanics of publishing journals are very different from book publishing and the early issues suffered the occasional hiccough; but these three journals, which for some years remained our only journals, moved nonetheless quite quickly into profit.

During the seventies there seemed to be a change in the pattern of school book buying which affected our own publishing programme. Teaching techniques appeared to be moving away from the course textbook towards a more eclectic approach, whereby teachers would have freedom to use a greater number of small books. At the same time school book funding was more generous than it had been (and far more generous than it was to become) so that schools were able to purchase sets of supplementary material.

Nicolas McDowall therefore published many small books, mainly in English, Religious Education and Social Studies, and for several years these were very successful. Good examples are Birnie: *Focus on Christianity, Checkpoints*, edited by John L. Foster (a series produced in newspaper format, dealing with subjects such as the handicapped, housing, and growing old), and the many English titles by Paul Groves and Nigel Grimshaw.

It was mentioned earlier that the Australian company became a wholly owned subsidiary in 1974. Under the new management service to customers improved, and sales of our tertiary books were satisfactory. Both of these elements were helped by the closure of the market in 1976; from then on, books were supplied to our Australian customers only through our own warehouse. However, publishing progress was slower than we had hoped, and the company was by no means always a positive contributor to the Group accounts.

In the United States we arranged for greater flexibility in the sale of our medical books, no longer channelling all titles through Williams and Wilkins. This resulted, for several years, in splendidly large sales of our more important new books, mainly through the Year Book Publishing Company in Chicago. Most of our humanities books were sold to University presses, particularly to Harvard, while scientific titles found a solid market through Halsted Press, a division of John Wiley run by Warren Sullivan.

Our long and fruitful relationship with the Macmillan Company of Canada received a setback when that company was sold to Maclean Hunter, the large journals group. The new owners, though not familiar with book publishing, made a sincere attempt to provide a good service for their agencies; but the expansive mood of the sixties had disappeared and, sadly, Canada ceased to be the significant market it had traditionally been.

In Japan we formed a new Macmillan relationship, moving our representation to their Japanese office in 1972. This flourished under the management of Yoshi Tadokoro, and Japan quickly became an important market for us, especially for medical books.

Last but not least, the middle seventies saw the beginning of the importance of Nigeria as a market. Sales had begun to develop earlier in the decade, but had been disrupted by the civil war. At this time both the management and the ownership of our agent, Pilgrim Books, were transferred to John Leigh, an able Sierra Leonian who had been a financial analyst with Ginn, by this time an educational publishing subsidiary of the Xerox Corporation. Sales began to increase substantially in 1977, but already showed indications of the problems which were to beset this market.

It will have become clear that since 1960 we had been active in all the worthwhile markets in the world, but that it was only in Australia that we were the sole owners of the outlet. The reason for this was, of course, that as a small company, with a wide and varied list to sell, we could not possibly afford to establish our own operation in all the important markets. Australia, too, had started as a consortium arrangement with George Bell and E. & S. Livingstone. This technique was applied to several different areas, and in almost all cases the consortium was administered in London by Arnold. This administration could include guidance over methods of representation and stockholding, and the organization of collective funds for financing the operation concerned. This could be time-consuming work, but the level of co-operation achieved by the publishers in each group was highly satisfying.

West Africa provided an early opportunity, when we worked with Evans Brothers and the Cambridge University Press; later with John Leigh, we joined forces with John Murray. East Africa, being a smaller market required a larger group. One of the largest of such arrangements was Book Promotions in South Africa. This was set up by John Morgan, after the death of Neville Chance in 1969. Neville's widow Brenda, who had been in the South African book trade, became the first managing director; she was succeeded by Richard Ross, and later by Roy Mansell. Book Promotions was purchased by the management in 1989 and continues to serve its former principals.

In India we had been represented for many years by Orient Longmans, but the expansion of our own list and the changing market in India led us to look for a method of working more closely with an Indian partner. Together with Heinemann Educational Books we found Gulab Vazirani; an agency, Arnold-Heinemann (India) was set up in 1969 and became a private limited company in 1973. Gulab Vazirani represented us from that time, and succeeded in maintaining a presence for Arnold in India in a very difficult period.

8

1978–1987

TOWARDS the end of 1977 it became obvious that another move in London was necessary. After six years of more or less uninterrupted expansion the Hill Street buildings were no longer large enough, and there was no means of finding additional accommodation close by. The search for premises which ensued was a great deal easier than in 1971, as the housing boom had been replaced by a prolonged property slump. We hit upon 41 and 42 Bedford Square with little delay, and the houses had already been repaired and decorated by the developer. They were about fifty years older than 25 Hill Street, but in many ways were similar; both the houses were rather smaller than the Hill Street one, but together they provided about 50 per cent more accommodation. Bedford Square was, of course, an ideal location for an educational publishing house, being so close to the British Museum, London University, major hospitals, and the Publishers Association. This was to be Edward Arnold's home for nine years until the sale of the company, and continued to be so subsequently, until the end of 1989.

These nine years started very well, for the Group's sales in 1978 increased by over 16 per cent on 1977, and despite the expenses of the move, profits exceeded half a million pounds. With the benefit of hindsight, however, it is clear that life became more difficult very shortly afterwards, with problems increasing after 1983. This chapter will try to show how these problems affected the company, and how they were eventually resolved.

Our school books were continuing to perform extremely well, and for some years their sales in the UK provided our largest and most profitable increases. The arrival of the Conservative government in 1979 produced an almost immediate change of climate, with severe cutbacks to the allowances for school-book funding. Several educational publishers had very difficult years at the beginning of the eighties, but our own school book sales held up well until 1983, with, for example, an increase in home sales of 18 per cent in 1981, and a further respectable increase in the following year. This was splendid, but with the continuing squeeze on expenditure, and the rapid introduction of the new GCSE examinations in 1985/86, the list began to suffer from a lack of solid and substantial textbooks. The small books, previously so successful, declined with alarming rapidity, while larger texts in the right areas, such as Peter Bishop's *Comprehensive Computer Studies*, sold in very large numbers.

One internal response to the cuts in educational spending was to increase the profile of our activities in Further Education. We had, of course been active in the field for many years, the books being subsumed in our school and science lists. It proved a good move to make a separate department for FE. This prospered, and though it derived much of its revenue from our established catering list it also broadened into other FE fields. One of its most successful books was Gross: *Psychology*, published in 1987 for the "A" level and first year university market. It reprinted within a month of publication, and had nine impressions in its first two years.

The difficulties in the market were by no means restricted to school books. Scientific publishing also suffered, textbooks and monographs alike. Biology had been the most rewarding market in science for a generation, but now the student numbers declined swiftly as jobs in industry and research were few and far between, and there was little for a biology graduate to do except teach other people biology. Fortunately a new and promising area had developed in the seventies in the shape of books for the computer market. John Roberts had made good progress with this, especially with some computer language books by D. M. Monro, so that by the start of the eighties we were established in the field. The ensuing boom in computer books had its pitfalls, especially in the home computer sector, and many publishers suffered horrific returns. This situation was skilfully handled by John Roberts, who concentrated almost entirely on Arnold's traditional textbook market. Advanced texts, such as D. R. Howe's *Data Analysis for Data*

Base Design were particularly successful, both at home and overseas.

Medicine, normally one of the most resilient of publishing areas, was not entirely exempt from the problems of the 80s. This was clearly shown in the effect on the various *Current Topics* series, which had formerly been successful; print runs became smaller, with a resulting increase in prices which further handicapped the sales. However, it was still possible to sell handsome quantities of books which were really something new, or just simply excellent. Paul Price published *An Introduction to the Symptoms and Signs of Surgical Disease* by Norman Browse in 1978, and in its first decade it sold about 75000 copies. New ground was also broken by some concise manuals, produced in a format to encourage the practitioner to keep it in his "white coat pocket". *A Manual of Neonatal Intensive Care* by N. R. C. Roberton was greeted with enthusiasm by *The Lancet* which suggested it "should be carried about by all those who regularly treat neonates". In addition to these new offerings there was, happily, a rich crop of new editions: *Mercer's Orthopaedic Surgery*, now edited by R. B. Duthie and G. Bentley, in 1983, *Greenfield's Neuropathology* in 1984, Clayton's *Obstetrics* and *Gynaecology* and Simpson: *Forensic Medicine* in 1985; and, most important of all, *Topley and Wilson's Principles of Bacteriology, Virology and Immunity*, the seventh edition of which was published in four volumes in 1983–84.

It is one of the privileges of being an academic publisher that one comes, not infrequently, into contact with very distinguished people. No one can have been more distinguished in his field than Sir Graham Wilson. Paul Price in particular, but also the present writer, experienced on many occasions not only his extraordinary clarity of thought, which some mistook for coolness, but also his great kindness and thoughtfulness. The very fine obituary in *Biographical Memoirs of the Royal Society* ends: "Men of his calibre are rare indeed, and his modesty in the light of his attainments was a source of wonder".

It was said earlier that the Humanities department published a large number of excellent books during the 70s; but towards the end of the decade the effects of over-optimistic publishing began to be noticeable. The new climate required that the selection of titles to be published should be made with great rigour. This was duly applied, but the recovery process was delayed by the fact that two heads of department, both talented, left for personal reasons after only a short time in office, thus destroying the continuity which is so important in academic publishing. By the middle 80s, however, the department, first under John Wallace and then under Christopher Wheeler, was beginning to produce a list of solid texts and reference books. In this they benefited from some excellent projects commissioned by Sarah Barrett. Good examples of this are, in history, A. J. Fletcher's *The Outbreak of the English Civil War*, and later volumes in *The New History of England*, notably Derek Hirst's *Authority and Conflict: England 1603–1658*; while in the field of language there were Michael Halliday: *An Introduction to Functional Grammar*, and *A Reference Grammar of Modern French* by Anne Judge and F. G. Healey – all of them books which will stay on the list for a long time.

A number of new journals were added to the list during this period, the two most interesting and promising being *Child Language Teaching and Therapy*, edited by David Crystal, and *Perfusion* (artificial circulation of the blood) under the editorship of Kenneth Taylor. Both these journals had the advantage of having very well-known and active editors.

In the mid 70s we felt that two lists which had grown out of the Education Department, the English Language Teaching list and the Overseas Publishing list, were capable of being further expanded. They also required a closer liaison with the marketing function in the territories relevant to them, and were therefore formed into a small Overseas department reporting to Bryan Bennett.

As ELT publishing needs specialist knowledge we appointed in 1977 Thérèse Tobin, an experienced EFL teacher, to run this list. As we could not provide the large investment required to produce and market multi-volume courses she concentrated on supplementary books, and built up a highly respected list in a variety of areas. Probably the most important of these is *An A to Z of English Grammar and Usage*, by Geoffrey Leech and others; it is becoming a standard grammar throughout the world. In our early discussions with Hodder & Stoughton we were interested to find that both sides realized the enormous potential of ELT, and the need to provide adequate muscle to compete in the field. We also found that, by chance, the two lists were neatly complementary.

Also in 1977, we appointed Nick Walker, now with the Melbourne University Press, to be our Overseas editor: he had had considerable experience in teaching abroad. The problems of this type of publishing, in some ways similar to ELT, are compounded by the risk of sudden, and sometimes fatal, changes in the market countries. We set out to offer a three-fold service: firstly to maintain the sales of our main list in countries which were rightly demanding their own syllabuses and books; secondly to reinforce this effort by publishing country-specific books to act as a spearhead to our sales drive: and lastly to help overseas companies with their own programmes and thus to forge links with them for future co-operation. A number of titles were successfully published for the Caribbean, and for Central and Southern Africa, but the main target was Nigeria. Some books, such as Jones: *Groundwork of Commerce*, were adapted for the West African syllabus, while others, for example, Clarke: *West Africa and Islam* were commissioned for the market. There were also a number of books in mathematics, science and English, which were published by African Universities Press, but edited and produced by Edward Arnold. This programme was beginning to be successful when, as will be seen below, the Nigerian economy collapsed, bringing the whole thing to a sudden halt.

Until the middle of the 80s Nigeria continued to be a very important and tantalising market. Sales to Pilgrim Books were large in 1978, but fell again in the following year. In 1981 they exceeded all expectations for not only was the normal business done through Pilgrim Books booming (and the payment situation was not too bad at this time) but the Nigerian government had made large sums of money available to the individual states, so that they could place additional orders. This resulted in a huge increase in business. We received an order from one of the smaller states for 5600 copies of a book on technical drawing. We felt it wise to query this; the reply, received by return, thanked us for pointing out the error, and stated that the quantity should have been 56 000. This order was supplied, and paid for quite promptly, but our experience with some of the other orders was less happy, and this eventually resulted in our having to write off a very large sum in the 1985 accounts. Trading continued on letters of credit, but in a much reduced and desultory fashion, so that, for the most part, the books we had commissioned and published specially for the market did not get far off the ground.

When considering the Australian market, our feelings that, in spite of some sales increases, we were not moving fast enough in the direction of publishing or real profitability led us to make a change in management. Robert Blackmore, formerly with Macmillan in Melbourne, made some positive contributions during his term of office, which lasted from 1979 to 1984. During this time we moved our offices and warehouse from their ramshackle premises in Bay Street, Port Melbourne to a very suitable building in Caulfield. We acquired an important new agency in the shape of W. W. Norton of New York, and this was largely due to an excellent presentation laid on in Melbourne. We also bought two small lists at reasonable terms, which provided us with some books to give our almost non-existent Australian list a degree of credibility. However, it became plain that we should never succeed in becoming a serious educational publisher under the existing regime; and as, to our way of thinking, the main point of having our own company in Australia was to do just that, another change became essential. After a further visit and many interviews we appointed Terry Coyle, who had previously been our sales director, and had run the company very effectively during a three month interim period. Shortly after this we also succeeded in appointing a capable and experienced educational publisher, who quickly began to lay the foundations of an interesting and viable list.

Around 1980 it also became far more difficult to sell our books in the United States. It remained, as always, relatively easy to sell good numbers of outstanding books; but for the many titles whose market in the States was formerly between 500 and 750 copies it was now hard to find a publisher. The reason was obvious: the Reagan administration was having a similar effect to our own Conservative government. Funding for education and libraries was reduced, so that a market of 750 copies became 500, 500 became 300, and these lower numbers were no longer a viable proposition for the importing publisher. At about this time Halsted Press, for years our principal customer for books in the physical sciences, ceased importing books from outside the John Wiley group. This situation worried us, for we found ourselves in the position of no longer being able to make adequate sales for some of our authors in the vital American market; and although all authors and most editors habitually overestimate the potential sale of their books in the United States, there is no denying its great importance. It therefore became necessary to find an alternative arrangement, and preferably one which would sell Arnold books in the United States under their own imprint, rather than that of the importing publisher.

A number of alternatives were examined early in 1982. At the end of a January visit University Park Press in Baltimore indicated they would like to come up with a proposal which they thought would come close to meeting our wishes. For about five years we had been selling books in biology and linguistics to this firm, so we knew them quite well. A meeting was arranged at which they spelt out an offer which had several attractions for us. We would be provided with office and warehouse facilities, to be paid for as a percentage of our sales made through the branch; all books would be sold on consignment under the Edward Arnold imprint; and Geoffrey Mann, already well known to us, would be appointed manager, and become a direct Arnold employee. Thus we were able to appoint as our man in America someone we knew and trusted, and who was familiar with our list; and to make a modest start in the States without any heavy capital expenditure. The Baltimore location was another attraction – convenient, a major port of entry, home to some friendly and helpful publishers, and with the further advantage that overheads were about two thirds of those in New York.

Following more meetings the Branch was established and started business on 1 July, 1982. The early years went extremely well. The turnover was inevitably small, as so many of our titles were out with other publishers, but sales naturally increased quite rapidly as more books were channelled through Baltimore. It was impressive, and much to the credit of Geoffrey Mann, that the Branch came very close to breaking even in 1984, its second complete year of trading.

This happy scene was thrown into a state of crisis in the spring of 1985 when University Park Press was abruptly put out of business by its parent company, Scott Foresman. This meant not only that we had very quickly to find our own premises, staff and computer, but also that we had to disentangle our business from that of UPP, who had been doing the billing. The first part of this was swiftly accomplished: excellent premises were taken in East Read Street, a computer was installed and one or two experienced clerical staff were taken on from UPP, to join Geoffrey and his promotional assistants. All this was extremely well done, but it did, of course, involve us in greater expense, and it diverted Geoffrey away from selling books and into administration. The loss from the unravelling of the business could have been very substantial, but with much persistent work from Geoffrey and from Jim Peck, and with considerable goodwill from Scott Foresman, the cost to us amounted to only $8000; the time lost was far more important than the money – as was the fact that our running costs could no longer be as low as they had been. In spite of this trauma the Branch's sales increased by 22 per cent in 1985, and made a further increase in 1986, at a time when our UK based trading was becoming stagnant; and although the Branch did not move into profit, the losses incurred were very small.

In 1985 a very interesting development occurred on the medical front. We had always attached great importance to the medical list, and these feelings were intensified during the lean times of the 80s. We began to consider actively how we might expand the list by acquisition, and our glance fell upon the small but distinguished firm of Lloyd-Luke. This had been founded, shortly after the Second World War, by Douglas Luke, and he and his wife Susan were highly and affectionately regarded in the world of medical publishing. The list contained some "plums", of the kind that all medical publishers covet, so the Lukes had naturally had many inquiries before we arrived on the scene. Perhaps our timing was right, or perhaps Douglas enjoyed the fact that we were also a small, British firm, and not normally given to acquisitive activities; at all events, after a few friendly discussions, the matter was settled, and Lloyd-Luke became part of our small group, with a guarantee that, although the imprint would become Edward Arnold, space would be found for the phrase "A Lloyd-Luke book". Among other titles we had acquired *Wiley and Churchill–Davidson's A Practice of Anaesthesia*, and, especially, *Clinical Chemistry in Diagnosis and Treatment*, by Joan Zilva and P. R. Pannall.

Some important changes of senior staff were made at this time.

Michael Soper and John Wallace joined the Board in January, 1985. Michael, who had been in charge of educational sales, became Head of the educational department, with Nicolas McDowall as senior editor. John Wallace, having for some years been in the humanities department, first as an editor, and then succeeding Sarah Barrett as Head, took charge of our tertiary sales and promotion. He had also been very successful on the personnel side. Both these new directors, appointed only two years or so before the sale of the company, made a fine contribution to the Board during this period.

In 1986 Jim Peck decided to leave us to become Financial Director of the Chatto, Virago, Bodley Head, Cape group. He had been with Edward Arnold for sixteen years and done many valuable things for the company. His successor, Tony Jarvis, came to us from the Oxford University Press with a wide commercial experience. His first interview was nearly a disaster, as we had been wrongly informed that Tony was a fully qualified chartered accountant. When it emerged, at once, that this was not so, Tony slyly suggested that as he was being interviewed under false pretences, he should leave forthwith. The meeting was, of course continued, and fortunately so, for Tony rapidly became indispensable and his performance during the next critical year or so was truly remarkable.

At this point it may be helpful to try to summarize the position in which we found ourselves at the beginning of 1986. After the healthy performance in 1978, referred to above, we experienced, like most other publishers, a fairly severe drop in profits in 1979; the sales increase in the UK was reduced by poor sales overseas, including Nigeria, while overheads, and particularly interest payments in that inflationary time, were going up. However, unlike many other publishers, we were able to improve this situation during the next year or two. In 1980 we had a large increase in sales, and an improvement in profits of about 14 per cent. 1981 saw very large sales to Nigeria, with our home turnover holding up well; profits climbed back over the half million mark. In 1982 our UK sales, including schoolbooks, continued to do well, but a poor year's exports resulted in an increase in group revenue of only 5 per cent, and a small decline in profits.

In 1983 sales to the African continent declined dramatically, but, more importantly, this was our first year of serious collapse in school book sales in the UK. Sales decreased marginally overall, and profits by more than half. 1984 was substantially better; excellent sales of medical books and good performances in Australia and the United States produced a revenue increase of 11 per cent and profits restored to some extent. 1985, however, was by far the worst year the company had experienced. Only a small increase was achieved in parent company sales, and a good performance in Australia was more than offset by adverse exchange rate movements, while, to add to our problems, it was necessary to write off a large sum for Nigerian debts. The best we could do was to achieve a technical break even.

This recital, dismal reading for the last part, will explain why, in 1986, we decided that we could no longer continue as an independent company; it is not necessary to explain that this decision was taken with very great reluctance. Interest in acquiring Edward Arnold had never ceased. Although it did not remain at the hectic level of the 60s, it was still a permanent feature of life, and never a Frankfurt Fair passed without one or two approaches, some civilized, some less so. One of these, enjoyable in its brevity, went something like this: "How would you like to sell Edward Arnold to a major American educational publisher not a million miles from Chicago?", "I would not." "Thank you."

Late in 1985 a more discreet player entered the field. Philip Attenborough had lunch with Bryan Bennett, whom he naturally knew as a result of Bryan's activities, particularly as Chairman of the Book Development Council. This led to Bryan and Anthony having lunch at Dunton Green early the following year, with Philip and Michael Attenborough and Richard Morris. This was a pleasant, exploratory occasion; nothing was pressed, but it was agreed to keep in touch. The lunch was in due course returned, and followed by a series of meetings, either in a restaurant, or in the H & S flat near Bedford Square, and all of which we were convinced were entirely secret. What emerged from these talks was a feeling on both sides that we could live together, and that there was a sound business logic for the merger. Arnold's need for such a move was abundantly clear, but Hodders also had good reasons for taking such a step. Five or six times the size of Edward Arnold, and very strong in general and paperback publishing, they had an educational division of good quality which was rather too small to make a powerful impact, in the market place or inside the group; acquisition of Edward Arnold would treble the size of Hodder's educational publishing.

We therefore moved quickly to an agreement in principle, which was announced in February 1987. A series of formal meetings ensued, which at the time seemed interminable; but in fact everything moved along quite rapidly, and the sale was completed on 6 May. Edward Arnold (Publishers) Ltd became Edward Arnold, the educational, academic and professional division of Hodder & Stoughton.

The changing faces of Edward Arnold.

9

1987–1990

D URING the negotiations one of the most important points
in the discussions had naturally been our wish to maintain
the identity of Edward Arnold as far as possible. As
independent publishers themselves, Hodder & Stoughton were
sympathetic and fair about this; it was agreed that the name should
remain, not only as an imprint, but also in certain other key areas,
at least until the end of 1988. An Edward Arnold Division was
formed, to consist of both Edward Arnold and the former H & S
Educational Division. This was administered by an Executive
Committee, consisting of Richard Morris as Chairman, Anthony
Hamilton as Managing Director, and Bryan Bennett and Brian
Steven. Most of the former Edward Arnold directors became
directors of the new division. This was divided into three publishing sections, each with a Managing Director: academic publishing
under Anthony Hamilton, international and vocational publishing
under Bryan Bennett, and schoolbook publishing – the largest
section – under Brian Steven.

It was clearly in the schoolbooks area that the two lists over-
lapped most closely, and it was agreed at the start that the two
schoolbook elements should be integrated under one roof, even
though this would have the unfortunate effect of separating the
schoolbook section from the rest of the division, since there was
not enough room in 41 and 42 Bedford Square to accommodate
the entire division. After some further discussion it was agreed
that the Arnold schoolbooks department should be located in the
Hodders offices at Dunton Green, near Sevenoaks, and this resulted
in the loss of a number of staff who did not wish to commute,
or to move from London. The other publishing departments,

however, remained in Bedford Square, and were joined by some people from the relevant departments in Hodders, among them Philip Walters, a divisional director of H & S, who became deputy to Bryan Bennett in the international and vocational section. Here the problems of integration were minimal.

The principal casualty of the acqusition was of course Woodlands Park; it was essential that savings should be made in distributive overheads, and that Arnold stocks should be moved to Dunton Green. Woodlands remained open until the end of 1987, with the staff gradually being run down as the business was transferred. This sad situation was made much less difficult than it might have been by Hodders, who came through at an early stage with a very fair financial offer to the staff. Their distributive and personnel directors formed a close and friendly relationship with Mike Husk, and made regular visits to Woodlands; and it should also be said that the Arnold staff at Woodlands behaved splendidly throughout this difficult time.

In Australia a smaller version of those events took place, with the distribution being absorbed by Hodders in Sydney, but the educational publishing remaining in Melbourne. In Baltimore the plan was similar, but it proved impossible to find an adequate replacement for Geoffrey Mann, who was anxious to return home to the UK; this, together with the problems attached to representing a fairly small, but wide list in the largest market in the world, resulted in the closure of the Branch during 1988.

Happily, several of our overseas agents, with whom Edward Arnold had had long and close links, were retained. Others, because of Hodder's existing commitments had eventually to cease, including Book Promotions in South Africa, and African Universities Press in Nigeria.

During 1987 substantial progress was made with the integration of the two companies, though there were, inevitably, a number of practical problems to be overcome. Firstly, there were several internal moves to be made, often of considerable complexity; these were quickly and quietly solved by the office manager, Alicia Goldberg. Then there were various systems, such as editorial committees, sales analysis and stock records, budgeting and costing procedures which had to be revised in order to fit in with the Hodder systems, which had been set up more for a trade list than for an educational and academic one. These problems naturally took a little longer to solve than the physical ones.

At the end of 1987 Anthony Hamilton retired; the company was extremely fortunate to be able to appoint Richard Stileman to take his place as Managing Director of the academic and professional side of the business. After a further six months, by which time the separate Arnold and Hodder lists in ELT, nursing and overseas publishing had been fully integrated, Bryan Bennett also retired. At that point it was decided that the Edward Arnold division should be re-organised from three sections to two: the educational and vocational lists under Brian Steven, to carry the Hodder and Stoughton imprint; and the academic, professional and overseas section, which now included the ELT, nursing and overseas lists, under Richard Stileman, continuing as Edward Arnold.

The central problem that faced the academic, professional and overseas section of Edward Arnold in 1988 and 1989 was a shortage of new publications. The books that were being published lived up well to the Edward Arnold tradition of quality, but there were simply not enough of them to justify the high overheads. As has been mentioned earlier, the mid 1980's was not a good time for editorial continuity and this was having its most marked effect in the latter part of the decade. A related problem was that books were still being published – albeit in small quantities – in a very wide range of subject areas. If each area was to be given due emphasis by the sales and marketing department, expenditure was bound to be excessively high.

The Baltimore branch office was particularly badly affected by these twin problems since the selling of academic and professional books in the USA is especially dependent upon economic use of specialist mailing lists and attendance – necessarily expensive – at conference exhibitions. The decision to close the Baltimore office in the summer of 1988 was made the easier by our being able to find excellent alternative outlets for all parts of the list. Routledge, Chapman and Hall Inc. of New York – formerly the US publishing and distribution arm of the scientific and academic imprints of the UK Group, Associated Book Publishers, but now part of the Canadian owned Thomson Corporation – were chosen for the humanities and science books, and Williams and Wilkins of Baltimore continued a long association with Edward Arnold by taking the medical backlist. It was decided that those new medical and engineering titles which had a good market in the USA would henceforth be co-published – a policy which has worked well on account of the inherent quality of the books being published and the excellent connections that exist between Edward Arnold and all the major American STM publishing houses. The closing of the Baltimore office was additionally facilitated by the decision of Geoffrey Mann to stay on until the bitter end.

Back home, there was a continuing need to adapt the amount and type of promotion and other selling activities – especially export – to the output of new titles and to the core of the backlist. This difficult task fell largely to Philip Walters, who was appointed Sales and Marketing Director in May 1988.

Towards the end of 1988, and into early 1989, we devoted much time to defining our publishing strategy for the future. The importance of the concept of "focus" was taken on board by all the editorial teams who each put forward plans demonstrating how they were going to publish enough quality material in each of their chosen areas of emphasis. For Edward Arnold as a whole one obvious area for expansion was medicine, where an excellent backlist and the prospects of closer links with *The Lancet* – also owned by Hodder & Stoughton – suggested scope for some exciting developments. A new Director – Nick Dunton, previously with John Wiley – was appointed to convert our ambitions into reality; Paul Price was appointed Chief Editor, and a third commissioning editor – Geoff Nuttall from Butterworths – joined in October 1989, thus making the team one of the strongest in the British Isles.

Chris Wheeler's Humanities team was also strengthened in 1989 with the arrival of Lesley Riddle thus at last providing a base from which it was hoped this area could escape its traditional problem of small scale. Our SET publishing under John Roberts, who left the company in June 1990 to be replaced by David Mackin, had a boost to its ambitions to publish a greater proportion of advanced books through the acquisition of Charles Griffin, primarily a publisher of statistics books and whose main legacy is the standard works of the late Sir Maurice Kendall. Changes to the organisation of our small journals publishing were made so as to encourage it not only to grow, but to grow in harmony with our book publishing interest.

But there were casualties too, and the decision at the end of 1988 of the Kenyan government to put a ban on school book imports finally put paid to our Overseas publishing which had already had to redirect itself after the Nigerian collapse in 1985.

At the very beginning of 1989 a most agonizing decision had to be taken. The high cost of 41 and 42 Bedford Square, and the operational difficulties of working 25 miles distant from the main Hodder & Stoughton offices had become increasingly apparent since the acquisition. But if we moved to Sevenoaks, would we lose so many of our staff that much of the reconstruction of the previous year would be wasted? We decided to take the gamble and between Christmas 1989 and the first days of 1990 we moved to a specially planned new extension at Dunton Green, into a working environment which has since proved both pleasant and highly efficient. Inevitably, we lost staff at the time of the move, several of them people who had given the company long and dedicated service. But the core of Edward Arnold remained intact and we only lost five (out of thirteen) commissioning editors, thus offering hope that our plans for publishing growth would be achieved with only the minimum of delay.

It is especially pleasing to reflect that in the year that inevitably closes this story, 1990, Edward Arnold looks healthy and strong after a decade of trauma. Although no longer an independent company, Edward Arnold nevertheless survives as an independent operating unit, with a jealously guarded imprint, within one of Britain's few remaining major independent publishing companies. The perfect conclusion to this story as well as the most fitting symbol for the future, is the publication in August of this year of yet another edition of Edward Arnold's most important work, Topley and Wilson's *Principles of Bacteriology, Virology and Immunity.*

Index